SACRAMENTO PUBLIC LIBRARY

D0174488

WHAT PEOPLE ARE SAYING ABOUT *IN THE GAP...*

In the Gap expresses the passion of a visionary leader who influences and inspires others to live and to die for God-given vision.

— Edwin Alvarez, Pastor of Comunidad Apostólica Hosanna in Panama City, Panama

If you want to learn how to be a person who stands for righteousness, who goes into the deepest valleys to be the light and the voice of truth, then read *In the Gap*. Pastor Choco inspires us with powerful examples of people throughout history who are Gap Leaders.

— Mark Batterson, *New York Times* best-selling author and Lead Pastor of National Community Church in Washington, DC

In the Gap is far more than an inspiring book about how to make a compelling difference. It's ideal for pastors to use in church-wide campaigns, or for class or small-group settings. Each chapter brings Bible characters into today's challenges with a fresh, engaging style. A self-assessment, discussion questions, and DVD offer additional practical uses. This is another winner from Pastor Choco!

— Warren Bird, coauthor of twenty-six ministry books including *Better Together: Making Church Mergers Work*

Pastor Choco's book is powerful. It challenges and empowers us to stand in the gap for our generations and communities. Pastor Choco is uniquely qualified to speak on this vital topic because he has literally stood in the gap for his community and the nation—and ultimately, he has stood in the gap for God's kingdom. I highly recommend Pastor

Choco's book to you. By reading it, you will walk away empowered to stand in the gap as I did when I encountered Pastor Choco's life!

— Russell Evans, Senior Pastor of Planetshakers City Church in Melbourne, Australia

In the Gap is a bold and daring challenge to stand strong and watch God work! Through the lives of great Bible heroes of yesterday, Wilfredo De Jesús challenges us to live more courageous lives today! If it's strength, bravery, or faith that you need, read this book! You can't read *In the Gap* without being inspired to live a more gutsy life for God!

— Dave Ferguson, Lead Pastor of Community Christian Church in Chicago, Illinois

This book identifies a tremendous need—it shows how God wants to use and equip us to be men and women who stand in the gap for the vulnerable in our society. This concept is crucial if we want to be like Jesus. If our communities hear us proclaim His good news, they also need to see the good news in action. And no one is better positioned to teach us how to do that than my friend, Pastor Choco. *In the Gap* reveals the heart of Choco's ministry, which is really the heart of Jesus' ministry.

— Dr. Tim Harlow, Senior Pastor of Parkview Christian Church in Orland Park, Illinois

There are few voices in a generation that have the authentic authority to call the army of the Lord to action. Pastor Wilfredo De Jesús is one of those voices. In his new book, *In the Gap*, De Jesús directs believers to stand up and stand strong. The message inspires and instructs, challenges and confronts, encounters and encourages. It is required reading for anyone determined to make a difference in the world.

— Dr. Chris Hill, Senior Pastor of The Potter's House of Denver, Colorado

I'm very excited about Pastor Choco's book, *In the Gap*. It will give you a fresh vision to reach the poor, the forgotten, and the oppressed in your community. You'll find practical steps to care for "the least of these" as you rediscover the heart of the gospel. Pastor Choco has stood in the gap for his city; now let's learn from the expert and follow his example to care for people in our communities!

— Rob Ketterling, Lead Pastor of River Valley Church, Apple Valley, Minnesota, and author of *Change Before You Have To*

Our world is full of "gaps"—places of weakness and vulnerability where we must stand on behalf of needy people and worthy causes. Pastor Choco reminds Christians of the call to stand in those gaps. He explores the traits of "gap people," holding up a mirror for us to examine ourselves. This book issues a much-needed challenge to the church, encouraging us to stand securely on Christ while we stand lovingly in the gap.

— Justin Lathrop, Director of Strategic Relations, Assemblies of God

Pastor Choco is a man of God who has lived out what it means to stand in the gap for others. This book will challenge you and inspire you to look around and make a difference.

— Pastor Clemente Maldonado, District Superintendent, Midwest Latin District of Assemblies of God

Every dreamer has a dream for others. It begins with a seed that flourishes into a harvest. Choco De Jesús is a dreamer who has always been the one to stand in the gap. In this great book, Choco reveals to us his lifelong strategy that has been a hallmark in his life. If you want to have your dreams fulfilled, this book is for you!

— Obed Martinez, Senior Pastor of Destiny Church in Indio, California

The church is called to be the hands and feet of the gospel in the broken world. In his new book, my friend and fellow pastor Wilfredo De Jesús challenges God's people to fill the gap between despair and joy in our communities. We need to hear this message, and then make it happen!

— Miles McPherson, Senior Pastor, The Rock Church, San Diego, and author of *God in the Mirror: Discovering Who You Were Created to Be*

In the Gap is a profound message written to answer the rising cry *within us* to impact the hurting society *around us*. Wilfredo De Jesús clearly, biblically, and inspiringly expounds the keys to respond to the gaps evident in the faces and families across America and the world. More than a book, *In the Gap* is the written proclamation to the cause we have all been called to join.

— Sergio De La Mora, Senior Pastor of Cornerstone Church in San Diego, California

The book you're holding will teach, inspire, and help you stand in the gap for someone. Pastor Choco can teach you how to do it because he has personally raised up an army of people in Chicago to stand in the gap for the hurting. You're about to change someone's life. You're about to become a stand-in-the-gap champion!

— Stephan K. Munsey, PhD, Senior Pastor of Family Christian Center in Munster, Indiana

Pastor Choco gives a clarion call to all of us to stand "in the gap" for those in need around us. This book will certainly inform you, but it will also inspire you to be the person Jesus has destined to stand in the gap for others. Jesus paid the price for us and has given us His Spirit—now it's time for us to stand in the gap for people in need.

— Benny Perez, Lead Pastor of The Church at South Las Vegas in Henderson, Nevada

Radical, revolutionary, innovative, anointed, and *cutting-edge* are words I use to describe Pastor Wilfredo "Choco" de Jesús. His new book reflects nothing less. *In the Gap* will challenge and inspire you to step out of your comfort zone, realign your priorities, take a radical stand for the less fortunate, and be creative with innovative ideas to reach your hurting community.

— Rev. J. R. Rodriguez, Superintendent, Texas Louisiana Hispanic District of the Assemblies of God

In his new book, *In the Gap*, Pastor Choco provides a biblical prescription that empowers the reader with the necessary tools to fill the areas in and around us left empty by sin, heartache, apathy, and relativism with grace, hope, and love. This book is a must read, indeed!

— Rev. Samuel Rodriguez, President, National Hispanic Christian Leadership Conference

Choco De Jesús is a powerful voice for God in challenging His people to fight for others. Unlike anyone else I know, he models this trait in his own life with the courage, faith, and inner strength of God. Now he's written a book that will stir you to do the same. Read *In the Gap* today, and prepare to be challenged!

— Stovall Weems, Senior Pastor of Celebration Church in Jacksonville, Florida

I am thrilled to read Pastor Wilfredo (Choco) De Jesús' new book, *In the Gap*. Not only is Choco a dear friend, but he is also a person I look up to and draw insight and spiritual strength from on a regular basis. As you read this book, I know that Jesus is reaching from heaven to take hold of your hand today. Quite often, He uses someone to stand in the gap who can touch Him while reaching out to rescue others who are too weak to reach up on their own. This book will help you stand in the gap for those who need Jesus.

— Rich Wilkerson, Senior Pastor of Trinity Church in Miami, Florida

Too many contemporary Christians seek lives of comfort and ease. But following Jesus Christ means ministering to others "in the gap," that is, in places of weakness, vulnerability, and danger. In this book, Pastor Choco highlights nine biblical heroes to show each of us how to become a "gap person." I highly recommend this book.

— George O. Wood, General Superintendent of The General Council of the Assemblies of God, USA, Springfield, Missouri

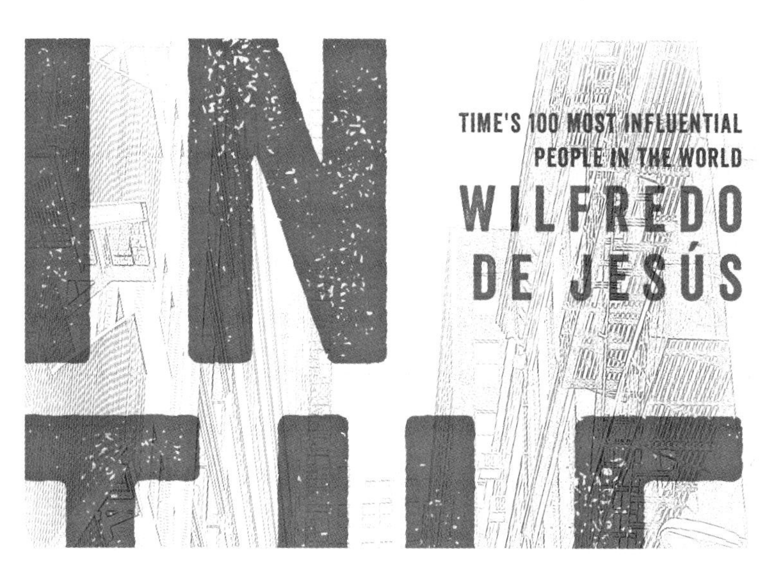

WHAT HAPPENS WHEN
GOD'S PEOPLE STAND STRONG

Copyright © 2014 by Wilfredo De Jesús

ALL RIGHTS RESERVED

Published by Influence Resources
1445 N. Boonville Ave.
Springfield, Missouri 65802
www.influenceresources.com

No part of this book may be reproduced, stored in a retrieval system, or transmitted in any form or by any means—electronic, mechanical, photocopy, recording, or otherwise—without prior written permission of the publisher, except for brief quotations used in connection with reviews in magazines or newspapers.

Cover design by Beyond Creative
Interior formatting by Anne McLaughlin, Blue Lake Design

Unless otherwise specified, Scripture quotations are taken from The Holy Bible, New International Version® NIV®. Copyright © 1973, 1978, 1984, 2011 by Biblica, Inc.™ Used by permission. All rights reserved worldwide.www.zondervan.com. The "NIV" and "New International Version" are trademarks registered in the United States Patent and Trademark Office by Biblica, Inc.™

ISBN: 978-1-93830-989-2

18 17 16 15 14 • 1 2 3 4 5

Printed in the United States of America

Note: In some stories, the names and details have been changed to protect anonymity.

I want to dedicate this book to the woman who has been with me longer than my mother—you guessed it, my lovely wife, Elizabeth. In my life and in our family, she is the quiet force behind the scenes making sure everything runs smoothly.

For the last thirty-five years, Elizabeth has led thousands of worship services—for her Dad when he was Pastor, and now for me. She has stood in the gap for true worship and has trained many worshippers throughout the years. Elizabeth has held the hand of God to worship Him in spirit and in truth. She believes that true worship is not a performance. She leads from the heart—the way God designed us to worship.

Elizabeth, thank you for your purity, thank you for standing strong, thank you for sharing your voice, thank you for your heart of worship, and thank you for being my wife and friend—te amo Mi Amor.

TABLE OF CONTENTS

ACKNOWLEDGEMENTS

First, I want to acknowledge my Father in heaven for His unconditional love and patience with me. To Him I dedicate my life. I will forever be grateful for the trust He has bestowed upon me with His bride and for providing me with the courage and strength to stand in the gap for her. I love you, Father.

I give a big "thank-you" to our church staff, board and elders who encourage, empower, and cover me and my family in prayer. You keep me moving forward and dreaming big. I sincerely appreciate your dedication and your commitment to serve the Lord. I'm forever grateful for your love and support.

I'd like to also say thank-you to the members of New Life Covenant Church and the younger generation who are learning what it means to be a gap leader. It's a privilege and an honor to pastor you. You are the greatest church in the world. I love you all.

To Influence Resources, especially Sol and Wini Arledge as well as Steve and Susan Blount, thank you for encouraging me to step out in faith again and put this book together. To my friend and writer, Pat Springle, who worked tirelessly to get this book out of my heart, thank you for sharing your awesome gift.

I want to acknowledge my brothers in Christ, Efrain, Rico, Deacon, Snake, Dino, and Izzy, who have stood in the gap with me in our city—and are still standing with me. Your loyalty and friendship mean the world to me. Thank you.

Finally, I want to acknowledge my entire family who has been a great blessing to Elizabeth and me as they, too, stand in the gap with me in the City of Chicago. To my amazing wife, Elizabeth, and our three beautiful children, Alexandria, Yesenia, Wilfredo Jr., and my son-in-law, Anthony, thank you for sharing your gifts and talents with the body of Christ. I am beyond grateful for your love and support. You are my greatest joy. I love you so much.

INTRODUCTION

Gaps All Around Us

"I looked for someone among them who would build up the wall and stand before me in the gap on behalf of the land so I would not have to destroy it, but I found none" (Ezek. 22:30).

A gap, by definition, represents a place of weakness, vulnerability, and danger. It is a defenseless location of exposure and limitation, a point where people face real threats. Gaps exist in our countries, our communities, and at home with our families.

In September of 1939, the German army launched an attack into neighboring Poland. Their strategy was revolutionary in the history of warfare . . . and the effects were devastating. The Panzers (German tanks) punched a hole in the Polish army's defensive wall. Then, the tanks, artillery, and infantry poured *through the gap* and attacked the defenders from the flanks and rear. The ferocity of the attack was so sudden and effective that it became known as Blitzkrieg, lightning war.

When an enemy attacks the gaps in our lives, we are hopelessly overwhelmed—if not for the grace of God and the intervention of His divine hand. As we read Scripture, we see how Moses stood in the gap for his people. Countless times, he pleaded for God to have mercy on his doubting, rebellious followers. At critical times, when the future of the people of God hung in the balance, Moses spoke to God for them and faithfully instructed them to follow God with all their hearts.

Centuries later, in about 590 BC, God's people were weak, vulnerable, and in danger. The mighty empire of Babylon threatened to attack Jerusalem and destroy Judah. The Jewish political leaders were terrified and turned on their own people. The religious elite used the chaos to gain power by lying to the people, and the common people committed crimes against each other. The poor, the needy, and the immigrants were mistreated. Even the weather caused heartache and calamity. Everything, it seemed, was going wrong for the people of God. In this chaos, God looked for someone He could trust, someone who would stand strong and represent His power, wisdom, and love. God's people desperately needed someone to stand up for them. Sadly, God had to report:

> "I looked for someone among them who would build up the wall and stand before me in the gap on behalf of the land so I would not have to destroy it, but I found none" (Ezek. 22:30).

In many ways, nothing has changed in two and a half millennia. People are still in distress, and God is still looking for men and women to stand in the gap in our homes, in our neighborhoods, in our cities and towns, in our nation, and in every corner of the world. Every news account tells us that people are in trouble. They are weak, vulnerable, and in danger. If no one stands in the gap for them, it will be a catastrophe. In many cases, a series of catastrophes have already occurred, and the gap is even wider.

This isn't a black or white problem, or a socio-economic problem. The problem isn't affecting some of us, but *all* of us. It affects our deepest hopes and fears. The gap looks like:

— a prodigal child,
— an unfaithful spouse,
— an abusive family member,
— an addict who is out of control,
— lying, stealing, and cheating,
— sexual promiscuity,
— parents who have lost hope for their kids,
— neighbors (even church members) who hate each other and poison their communities,
— gangs, violence, and other crimes,
— the elderly who are forgotten and overlooked,
— children who grow up unable to read,
— poverty from lack of training and skills,

— social breakdown, including human trafficking, attacks on the sanctity of marriage, racism, immigrants lost in the system, prostitutes and others who have made terrible choices and feel cut off from the goodness of God.

Do you recognize any of these gaps around you right now? You may have protected yourself and your family from many of them, but all of these life-threatening problems are only minutes away from all of us—and many of us live with these difficulties all day every day.

Huge gaps have opened up in our world. Do we even notice? Do we care? God is asking, "Will you stand in the gap for these people? Will you stand in the gap for My sake and My glory?"

What is a "gap person"? Who is the kind of person God is looking for, the type of man or woman, young or old, who has insight into the problem and courage to take bold action. God isn't looking for people who feel no fear. He's looking for people who walk toward their fear and stand in the gap to help those in need.

The Bible uses a Hebrew term to describe the kind of person who stands in the gap for others: *ish habinayim*. *Ish* is a man; *isha* is a woman. *Habinayim* is "one who places himself between the two camps and offers single combat."[1] The effort involved means to break or burst out, like a child coming out of a womb, to break through, break open, or break the limits of a stronghold. So, an *ish* (or *isha*) *habinayim* is a champion for a cause, a person who protects or supports someone in need, a man or woman who finds the courage to sacrifice everything to represent God and block evil from destroying those He loves.

When we look at the Scriptures and the history of God's people, we find at least nine traits that characterize "gap people." Particular people found in the pages of the Bible exemplify each of these:

- Nehemiah identified a problem to solve,
- Esther understood her times,
- Noah was "all in," no matter what the cost,
- David was anointed by God to do the work,
- Barnabas saw hidden potential,
- John the Baptist was willing to take risks,
- Gideon was sensitive to the voice of God,
- Deborah earned a reputation of wisdom and strength, and
- Caleb had "a different spirit."

All of us have the privilege and the responsibility to stand in the gap for those around us. Love, courage, and tenacity, though, don't come out of a vacuum. We look at Jesus. John the Baptist told people, "Look, the Lamb of God, who takes away the sin of the world!" (John 1:29) When we look at Him—and begin to realize the wonder of His awesome power and consistent

"Random acts of kindness" are wonderful, but most needy people have complex problems that aren't solved easily or quickly.

love—our hearts are transformed. The message of the gospel never gets boring. When we were weak, vulnerable, and in danger, Jesus stepped out of the comfort and glory of heaven to give, not just His time, but His life for you and me. He didn't just risk His reputation; He poured out His blood for us. We were broken sinners, but Jesus loved us so much He gave it all to pay the ransom to bring us back home to God.

People who are in desperate need may have nothing to offer us in return for our care. That's how Jesus loves us—unconditionally—and that's what it means for us to love people in need. His story of the good Samaritan demonstrates what it means to stand in the gap for someone. We need to notice—to see others' needs: spiritual, physical, relational, and emotional. Our hearts need to be soft enough to feel the pain of others and strong enough to care. Compassion is one of the marks of a person who stands in the gap. And like the good Samaritan, we need a plan. "Random acts of kindness" are wonderful, but most needy people have complex problems that aren't solved easily or quickly. The word *compassion* means "with passion." It's easy to be passionate about our careers or our education or even our entertainment but what about our passion for the poor? When we encounter hurting, struggling people, we need to resist the temptation to pass by on the other side of the road, assuming that "it's not my problem." We need enough passion to actually reach out to help a person.

The story of the good Samaritan shocked those who heard Jesus that day. It was inconceivable that a foreigner—Jews despised the Samaritans—would go out of his way to show such care to a Jew who had been attacked by thieves. And of course, Jesus is the ultimate good Samaritan. He was a foreigner—not from another nation, but from another realm. He stepped out of the glory of heaven to earth, cared for the helpless and hopeless, and paid the price we could never pay for our freedom, healing, and purpose.

When we consider becoming people who stand in the gap, we must draw on the love, power, wisdom, and example of One who stood in the gap for us.

Why are we hesitant to stand in the gap for those in need? There are many reasons. We don't want anyone to take advantage of us. We have our own priorities of comfort and pleasure, and we don't want the inconvenience. We fear that people will think we're weird if we invest our time and hearts in the lives of those who can't give us anything in return. We may be fearful that if we pour ourselves out for others, God will leave us empty and alone. Selfishness and fear—these are the most common reasons we're reluctant to stand in the gap for hurting people around us.

The people we'll examine in this book, and the men and women today who stand in the gap in their families and communities, believe in a God of awesome power, strong love, and infinite wisdom. In spite of the complexities of their situations, they trust God is greater—far, far greater—than the problems people face. Out of hearts filled with God's kindness and strength, they pour themselves out to mend broken hearts, restore relationships, and rescue the souls of the people they find on the side of life's road.

In the days before Jesus was betrayed, arrested, tortured, and killed, He explained what it means to be a gap person. He told what will happen when the Son of Man sits on His glorious throne and considers the people before him. One group will be those who saw others in need—hungry, thirsty, strangers, naked, sick, and in prison—but didn't bother to help them. The other group will be those who went out of their way to care for misfits and outcasts. The King will be pleased with them and will say to them:

> "Come, you who are blessed by my Father; take your inheritance, the kingdom prepared for you since the creation of the world. For I was hungry and you gave me something to eat, I was thirsty and you gave me something to drink, I was a stranger and you invited me in, I needed clothes and you clothed me, I was sick and you looked after me, I was in prison and you came to visit me" (Matt. 25:34–36).

The people will ask, "Lord, when did we see you hungry and feed you, or thirsty and give you something to drink? When did we see you a stranger and invite you in, or needing clothes and clothe you? When did we see you sick or in prison and go to visit you?" (Matt. 25:37–39)

The King will smile and reply, "Truly I tell you, whatever you did for one of the least of these brothers and sisters of mine, you did for me" (Matt. 25:40).

The astounding truth Jesus taught was this: When we stand in the gap for hurting, discouraged people who are often difficult to love, He considers that we're actually pouring out our love on Him. And nothing pleases Him more!

There are many good motivations to be a gap person. We're being obedient to God's command, He pours out His Spirit on us, and we see lives changed. But perhaps the most compelling motivations are that we represent and resemble Jesus when we pour our lives out for others, and that makes Him proud.

In the chapters of this book, we'll explore the nine traits of people who stand in the gap to care for others. At the end, you can take the questionnaire to see where you're strong (and perhaps where you need some improvement) as you stand in the gap.

Every Sunday before we sit to hear the Word of God, we make this confession of faith and commitment. As we begin, let's make this same confession.

Your Word is written in my mind.
Your Word is hidden in my heart.
Your Word is a lamp unto my feet and a light to my path.
I will seek you with all my strength.
I choose to live my life according to your Word.
Your Word, O Lord, is eternal.

May the God of grace, wisdom and power fill you with His Spirit and give you courage to stand in the gap for those around you!

1 NEHEMIAH

. . . identified a problem to solve

"So we rebuilt the wall till all of it reached half its height, for the people worked with all their heart. But when Sanballat, Tobiah, the Arabs, the Ammonites and the people of Ashdod heard that the repairs to Jerusalem's walls had gone ahead and that the gaps were being closed, they were very angry" (Neh. 4:6–7).

Exile. It's a word that most people in America today can't really understand. When people are exiled, what is most important is taken away: security, familiarity, comfort, and relationships. They're torn from everything they know and love, and they're forced to live in a foreign land. In an era of rapid transit and world travel, foreign lands are more accessible than ever before, but vacationing in another country is nothing like being exiled. We can't begin to imagine the conditions of a barren camp for refugees. Enslaved and separated from any social network, exiles lack sufficient food and water, have no protection from harsh weather, and are exposed to sickness and disease from filthy and overcrowded living quarters. The life of a displaced refugee is fearful and lonely.

When the Babylonians defeated Judah in 586 BC, they destroyed the temple in Jerusalem, stole the golden vessels from the altar, and took most of the captured people back to Babylon. It was a forced march. There are ancient images of men and women being dragged along dusty roads with fish hooks in their noses. The physical and emotional pain was excruciating, but the destruction of the temple broke their hearts. For centuries, God's people had worshipped there in the presence of God. His *shekinah* glory dwelled in the holy of holies in the innermost part of the temple. Miracles happened every day. No matter which way the wind blew, the smoke from the sacrifices always went straight up to heaven. In the fields, God gave them a bumper crop in the sixth year so they could take the next year, a sabbatical year, off from their labors.

Now, all that was gone. Jerusalem was destroyed. The temple was torn down and looted, and about 50,000 inhabitants stumbled into exile in Babylon . . . including Ezekiel.

After many years, God's people began to return to their homeland. Zerubbabel and Ezra led the first group. They restored the altar, the sacrifices, and worship of God. About twenty years later, a new temple was built and dedicated. During this period, the Persians conquered Babylon. Nehemiah was a Jewish man who had remained in Persia. His story begins 141 years after the fall of Jerusalem. He rose to a place of honor as the cupbearer to King Artaxerxes.

YESTERDAY AND TODAY

Before we continue with Nehemiah's story of courage, we need to understand something about ancient culture and biblical truth from the Old and New Testaments. The temple was the place where heaven and earth met, the place where God dwelled in His awesome glory. The wall around the city protected the temple. God's people couldn't imagine their temple being destroyed by a foreign army that worshiped foreign gods. But it happened because they became too self-absorbed, full of doubts, greed, and fear.

At the moment Jesus died on the cross, the heavy veil separating the holy of holies from the rest of the temple ripped apart from top to bottom. Why is this significant? The curtain no longer separated the people from God. Because of Christ's supreme sacrifice, God's presence and His glory no longer reside in a building. They reside in His people. One of the amazing truths of the New Testament is that you and I are temples of the Holy Spirit. Paul wrote to the people in Corinth: "Do you not know that your bodies are temples of the Holy Spirit, who is in you, whom you have received from God? You are not your own; you were bought at a price. Therefore honor God with your body" (1 Cor. 6:19–20). We are the place where heaven and earth meet! And we need to build walls of protection to defend and cherish God's glory in us—walls of integrity, obedience, faith, hope, and love.

So, when we read about the events that occurred in Nehemiah's life so long ago, we can make specific applications in our own lives. All around us, the enemy attacks people, but some are too absorbed with doubt, greed, and fear to fight back. Their temple is ransacked, and their walls torn down. Sometimes, it's not just our family members, friends, or co-workers who are devastated. Sometimes it's us.

God is always looking for someone to stand in the gap. About 141 years after Jerusalem fell to the Babylonians, God's people were still in distress. They were victims of injustice and racial hatred. The walls of the city lay in ruins. It was like living in a house without walls to protect them and to keep them warm. At this moment, Nehemiah answered God's call.

THE REPORT

Nehemiah had a dream job. He was the king's right-hand man . . . trusted, important, respected by everyone in the kingdom. By this time, the Jews living in Persia weren't the ones who had been led away by fishhooks through their noses. That was long, long ago, almost as distant in time as the Civil War in this country. The Jews had made a home in Babylon and Persia, and at least a few of them had positions of prominence. Their great-great-great grandparents had been pitiful exiles, but after many years living there, they had made Babylon their home.

Nehemiah was just as settled into his role as we might be if we had a prestigious position in our city or our nation. One day in the capital city of Susa, he saw Hanani, one of his brothers, who had just come back from Judah, which was 766 miles away. Nehemiah asked what was going on back in their homeland. He might have expected his brother to say, "Not much," or "Things are fine." He didn't. He reported that the people of Jerusalem were in big trouble. Outsiders were harassing the citizens, raping the women, and stealing from the people—and no one could do anything about it.

HE PRAYED

With revelation comes responsibility, and for Nehemiah, hearing this news broke his heart. But he didn't jump to conclusions or act impulsively. Many of us get the sequence wrong. For us, it's "fire, ready, aim!" Nehemiah's heart was shattered, but he knew he needed to prepare before he acted.

For days, he wept, fasted, and prayed. The condition of God's people in their homeland was simply unacceptable to him. God gave Nehemiah a holy discontent, a fire in his bones to make a difference. His prayer wasn't an outburst of anger and self-pity. He didn't demand anything from God. Instead, he focused his heart on the greatness and grace of God. He didn't blame "those people" for the problem. Though Nehemiah was hundreds of miles away, he identified with the people who were suffering. He included himself in the group that needed God's cleansing forgiveness. His prayer teaches us three steps to humbly make a request of God.

1. He acknowledged God (praise),
2. He reminded himself (and God) of the covenant He had made with His people, and
3. He confessed his sins and the sins of the people.

Only then did Nehemiah lay his request at God's feet:

> "Lord, let your ear be attentive to the prayer of this your servant and to the prayer of your servants who delight in revering your name. Give your servant success today by granting him favor in the presence of this man" (Neh. 1:11).

If you don't want to find out what's really going on in the life of an individual, a family, or a community, don't ask. You might discover a problem that's making people "distressed and downcast, like sheep without a shepherd." Nehemiah shows us another important trait: When the pain others feel breaks your heart, don't act impulsively. Of course, imminent danger requires immediate action, but in most cases, we need to follow Nehemiah's example to spend time getting the Father's perspective through persistent prayer. Prayer is a weapon against the schemes and attacks of the enemy. It's a channel of God's incredible blessings. It puts us in touch with God's heart, His power, and His grace. This kind of prayer isn't reserved for the super-spiritual saints, missionaries, or pastors. God invites all of us to seek His face. Nehemiah wasn't a prophet, a priest, or a Levite. He was an ordinary man with an extraordinary heart for God. When Nehemiah heard about the shattered walls and the abused people of his homeland, he didn't walk away in apathy, find a friend to have a pity party, or throw his hands up in despair. He put his hands together in fervent prayer to the God who gives wisdom, hope, and power . . . the God who can move a mountain . . . the God who can move the heart of a pagan king.

Prayer is a weapon against the schemes and attacks of the enemy. It's a channel of God's incredible blessings.

HE PLANNED

For Nehemiah, prayer was preparation for action. In the National Football League, the referees give teams twenty-five seconds after one play ends before the next time the ball is snapped. Both teams, the offense and the defense, use this time in their huddles to call their plays and get the right players on the field. Then, the quarterback and the defensive captain say,

"Break!" It's time for action. Every player knows that when he hears "break" that it's a call to duty, a call to act and implement the plan. Every pastor, leader, teacher, and disciple has similar calls to action. At specific times and places, they need to move past their fears toward what God is calling them to do. Prayer is our time to huddle, to get plays from our heavenly Coach, and prepare to take bold action. Too often, people think prayer is the ultimate goal, not preparation to act. As an excuse to avoid hard decisions, some people tell me, "Pastor, I'm still praying about that." Don't get me wrong. I'm all for prayer. We desperately need to tap into the wisdom and strength of God so we'll be ready to do what He calls us to do. But that's the point: God has called us to *do* something!

We desperately need to tap into the wisdom and strength of God so we'll be ready to do what He calls us to do.

Nehemiah prayed, and his prayer led to his plan. He knew the only person who had the authority to provide the resources to rebuild the walls of Jerusalem was King Artaxerxes. A few days later, as Nehemiah was serving him, the king noticed that he was preoccupied. The king had never seen his trusted servant like this, so he asked, "What's wrong?"

Nehemiah realized the moment of truth had come. He was terrified, but his fear didn't stop him. He replied with respect and boldness: "May the king live forever! Why should my face not look sad when the city where my fathers are buried lies in ruins, and its gates have been destroyed by fire?" (Neh. 2:3)

Persia wasn't a democracy. Artaxerxes was the most powerful and feared man in history. He had absolute power over his nation and his people. In our country, we have town hall meetings to complain to our elected officials, and we write or say anything we want to about them. In ancient Persia, any hint of disappointment in the king might mean instant death! Nehemiah took a real risk by voicing his concerns. To his great relief, the king answered, "What is it you want?"

Instead of blurting out his request (which is what most of us would have done), Nehemiah prayed silently before he opened his mouth. At that pivotal moment, he stayed connected to God, the ultimate source and resource. He then told the king, "If it pleases the king and if your servant has found favor in his sight, let him send me to the city in Judah where my fathers are buried so that I can rebuild it" (Neh. 2:5).

The king gave Nehemiah everything he needed: letters of safe conduct to travel, timber for the beams of the gates, and time away to get the job done. Nehemiah commented, "And because the gracious hand of my God was on me, the king granted my requests" (Neh. 2:8). He never lost sight of the fact that even the most powerful people on the planet are tools in the hands of Almighty God.

Years ago when we were about to embark on a missions trip to the Dominican Republic, I was made aware that Santo Domingo needed ambulances. I saw the mayor of the city of Chicago, Mayor Daley, at a press conference, and I took the opportunity to share the need. I asked if the city could donate two ambulances to this poor country. To my surprise, in a few days I received the response that the mayor had authorized the donation of two ambulances.

If you're experiencing a great difficulty, and you're ready to undertake a great work, then you need the power of a great God.

Now we just had to figure out how to get them to Santo Domingo. I went to the mayor again and requested a letter for safe passage across state lines. We needed to drive the ambulances to Miami where they would be loaded on a cargo ship. Mayor Daley granted my request. I saw his answer as scripture coming to life. Asking for a letter from a leader of a major city posed a risk. He could have felt bothered, and he could even have retracted his donation of the ambulances. But I knew God was with me, and that it was His job to work in the heart of this man. All I needed to do was ask.

Nehemiah understood a profound truth: If you're experiencing a great difficulty, and you're ready to undertake a great work, then you need the power of a great God.

Nehemiah exemplified the "gap person trait" of being able to identify a problem, then craft a plan to meet it. He didn't just hope the problem would go away. He didn't push it off on someone else. Nehemiah felt the weight of the responsibility to rebuild the devastated walls of the capital of his ancient homeland. During his days of prayer and fasting, God gave him direction to ask the king for all the resources. The request was simple enough, but it was full of danger. He was risking his life, and if he failed, God's people would continue to suffer from attacks and injustice in Jerusalem.

HE PROCEEDED

King Artaxerxes must have loved and trusted Nehemiah. He not only gave his cupbearer all the resources he needed to rebuild the crumbled walls; he also sent his cavalry with Nehemiah as an escort to protect him. Nehemiah led them 766 miles, but the journey took a few detours, possibly to Lebanon, to cut huge cedar trees for timber for the gates.

Imagine the scene: The right-hand man of the most powerful ruler on earth shows up at your devastated city with hundreds of cavalry soldiers in their finest uniforms, dragging wagons of huge logs. If you're a citizen of Jerusalem, you don't know what to think! Is the king's man coming to oppress you or help you? Is he friend or foe?

Nehemiah didn't tell anyone about his vision or his plans. Under cover of night, he inspected the city and the remains of the walls. On horseback in the dark, he secretly examined the southern walls to check their condition. Traditionally, Jerusalem had been attacked from the north. He probably assumed the northern parts of the wall were completely destroyed. For over 140 years, they had been no more than mounds of crumbled stone.

Before he announced his plans and called people to action, he wanted to know the extent of the problem. Finally, after three nights of reconnaissance, he called Jerusalem's priests, nobles, officials, and people together. He told them, "You see the trouble we are in: Jerusalem lies in ruins, and its gates have been burned with fire. Come, let us rebuild the wall of Jerusalem, and we will no longer be in disgrace" (Neh. 2:17). He told them the whole story of Hanani's report, his prayer, his request of the king, and the king's gracious answer. He wanted them to know this wasn't just something he had dreamed up. It was God's idea, and he was God's messenger and servant. Nehemiah was inviting them to join him in a great work.

They replied, "Let us start rebuilding" (Neh. 2:18). They put on their tool belts, grabbed their work gloves, and looked to Nehemiah to give them directions.

HE PERSUADED

Some people are so negative they can find fault with a bowl of ice cream. No matter what good things are going on around them, they are messengers of darkness. They have a spiritual gift—the gift of discouragement! Immediately, Sanballat the Horonite, Tobiah the Ammonite, and Geshem the Arab mocked Nehemiah and the men who agreed to help him rebuild the walls. These men had a vested interest in keeping God's people weak and vulnerable. They were gap people—but they didn't stand in the gap; they exploited it!

They made the most serious accusation against Nehemiah, one that would have made the workers shudder. They asked, "Are you rebelling against the king?"

Treason was punishable by death . . . often a long, slow, painful death. I can imagine the people looking at each other and wondering, *Uh, are we sure this Nehemiah has permission to do all this? If not . . . we're in deep trouble!*

Nehemiah didn't back down an inch. I can almost see him stand up straight as he boldly and loudly answered their charge. He could have told them that King Artaxerxes had given them permission, but the presence of the cavalry already made that clear. Instead, he claimed a higher authority: "The God of heaven will give us success. We his servants will start rebuilding, but as for you, you have no share in Jerusalem or any claim or historic right to it" (Neh. 2:20).

That was enough. The people were persuaded that Nehemiah had all the authority he needed to lead them. He had met the first test with courage.

FACING CHALLENGES

Standing in the gap involves difficulties and invites opposition. When you reach out to help a prodigal child, an addict, a homeless person, someone who is depressed, or a person who is chronically unemployed, things often get messy. When you confront gangs and racial injustice in your community, you can expect opposition and real danger. The three men who accused Nehemiah of treason illustrate three different challenges.

Standing in the gap involves difficulties and invites opposition.

Compromise

Sanballat's name means "may sin come to life." He was the governor of Samaria, a region north of Jerusalem. When the Northern Kingdom of Israel fell to the Assyrians in 722 BC, some Jews stayed behind in Samaria. They intermarried with their pagan conquerors and formed a new life. When Zerubbabel, Ezra, and Nehemiah came back from Babylon to restore the nation, the Samaritans, including Sanballat, felt threatened. They opposed resettlement because the returning exiles would upset their new world. The hatred between Jews and Samaritans started then, and it continued during the time of Jesus.

The Samaritans had bent their lives, their standards, and their faith to accommodate the pagans among them. It may have begun gradually, but after a few years, the Jews there had lost their distinctive faith and culture. Today, the world is still trying to bend us to their way of life. They insist, "It's no big deal. Everybody's doing it." So we make tiny, incremental choices to bend God's best for sex, truth, money, time, and relationships. Like the frog in a kettle, the heat keeps getting turned up, but it happens so slowly that we don't even notice—until we're boiled in sin!

People in the world look at Christians who love Jesus and are serious about their faith, and they shake their heads, "For crying out loud! Can't these people lighten up a little? They need to learn to have a little fun!" Yes, sin is fun for a season, but sooner or later, it takes a bite . . . and then devours.

When Sanballat attacked Nehemiah, he used a whip and a hammer. He asked sarcastic, demeaning questions, and he brought an army. In both ways, he tried to intimidate Nehemiah and his workers. Nehemiah records:

> "When Sanballat heard that we were rebuilding the wall, he became angry and was greatly incensed. He ridiculed

> the Jews, and in the presence of his associates and the army of Samaria, he said, 'What are those feeble Jews doing? Will they restore their wall? Will they offer sacrifices? Will they finish in a day? Can they bring the stones back to life from those heaps of rubble—burned as they are?'" (Neh. 4:1–2)

If you want to stand in the gap for people in your family or your community, some people will ridicule you, mock you, and try to intimidate you. Your courage and faith threaten them, so they'll do anything they can to make you compromise. If they can get your faith to slip, they'll mock you even more. No, none of us is perfect. We're all flawed, and God isn't finished with us yet. But our task is to hold on tenaciously to Christ, to trust Him for wisdom and strength, and to stand strong against the temptation to compromise our ethics, the truth, and the vision God has given us.

Division

Tobiah was an Ammonite, a pagan, yet his name means "God is good." Even though we might assume that his name meant he would support Nehemiah, he opposed him. Every time Tobiah's name was spoken, it was like a stone in a shoe: it caused the Jews to flinch! Everywhere he went, Tobiah caused resentment, confusion, and division. Centuries before, when God instructed His people to conquer the Promised Land, He told Joshua and his soldiers to wipe out the Ammonites. Instead, God's people compromised and failed, so the Ammonites continued to harass them.

Tobiah governed the area around Jerusalem. Nehemiah was rebuilding God's city right under his nose! His reaction was to create doubt and sow discord between the people and Nehemiah. Tobiah shouted so the workers could hear him, "What they are building—even a fox climbing up on it would break down their wall of stones!" (Neh. 4:3)

He was trying to say, "Nehemiah's plans are terrible, and his building technique is poor. All this work is for nothing! And besides, Nehemiah isn't even from around here. What are you doing following him?"

When work on the walls proceeded and success was in sight, opposition intensified. Sanballat, Tobiah, the Arabs, and the Ammonites were furious. They plotted to attack Nehemiah and his men. Nehemiah responded as a great leader: he prayed and posted guards to protect the city. He put men with swords and spears with their families. He was sure they would be more diligent and fight more ferociously to protect those they loved. From that time forward, half of the workers built the walls while the other half stood guard with spears, shields, bows, and armor. Each of the men, even those who were working on the wall, carried a sword on his hip.

For us, division comes in two forms: internally and externally. Our enemy tries to create *a divided heart,* to tempt us to pursue things that aren't God's best. The lure of power, control, and comfort can steal our hearts. It's not that these things are inherently wrong. They're often God's gifts to us. But when they take first place in our hearts, they split our attention and our allegiance. Like David, we need to pray, "Teach me your way, LORD, that I may rely on your faithfulness; give me an undivided heart, that I may fear your name" (Ps. 86:11).

Our enemy also wants to create *division between people*. Conflict isn't the problem; unresolved conflict is. It's normal for people to disagree and even to have their feelings hurt from time to time. When they can be honest with each other, forgive and restore, the relationship can be stronger than ever. Unhealed wounds, unfounded gossip, unforgiven sins, and unrelenting resentment drive a deep wedge that can't be smoothed over by a smile and a "God bless you."

Unhealed wounds, unfounded gossip, unforgiven sins, and unrelenting resentment drive a deep wedge that can't be smoothed over by a smile and a "God bless you."

Paul wrote the Christians in Galatia, "You, my brothers and sisters, were called to be free. But do not use your freedom to indulge the flesh; rather, serve one another humbly in love. For the entire law is fulfilled in keeping this one command: 'Love your neighbor as yourself.' If you bite and devour each other, watch out or you will be destroyed by each other" (Gal. 5:13–15).

When we try to stand in the gap to help those in need, we can expect the threats of division—in our hearts and in our relationships. Winston Churchill once observed, "You have enemies? Good. That means you've stood up for something, sometime in your life."[2]

Storms

Geshem's name means "storms," the kind of heavy rains that drench the ground in the fall and winter in that region of the world. Storms blow up unexpectedly and can cause devastating erosion of the land. Remarkably, Geshem is the only person in the Bible identified as an Arab.

Nehemiah and the workers finished the walls with incredible speed, but before they could build and hang the gates, Sanballat and Geshem again tried to stop them. They used threats, intimidation, and distraction, but Nehemiah saw through all their deceptions. Then, they used their final ploy. Nehemiah tells us,

> "One day I went to the house of Shemaiah son of Delaiah, the son of Mehetabel, who was shut in at his home. He said, 'Let us meet in the house of God, inside the temple, and let us close the temple doors, because men are coming to kill you—by night they are coming to kill you.'
>
> But I said, 'Should a man like me run away? Or should

> someone like me go into the temple to save his life? I will not go!'" (Neh. 6:10–11)

Geshem and his allies weren't playing games. Storms are destructive. We may see hurricanes, tornadoes, and tsunamis featured on the Weather Channel, but other kinds of storms—addiction, abuse, abandonment, poverty, depression, sex slavery, prostitution, loneliness, shame, and hopelessness—destroy individuals, families, and whole communities. For Nehemiah and for us, a half-completed wall isn't enough protection. We need to finish the work, no matter what it takes. Miraculously, Nehemiah and his men completed the work to rebuild the walls of Jerusalem in only fifty-two days. They had been lying in ruins for 141 years, but Nehemiah stood in the gap, identified a problem, created a plan, and completed the job God gave him to do.

> God didn't protect him from *experiencing* the storms, but He gave Nehemiah and his men courage to *weather* the storms.

I don't know how many times Nehemiah got discouraged, but he kept looking to God for hope and strength. I don't know how many people complained about all the work, but Nehemiah just smiled and said, "Keep working. God is with us." I don't know how many lies were told about him, but he trusted God with his reputation. The storms were fierce. God didn't protect him from *experiencing* the storms, but He gave Nehemiah and his men courage to *weather* the storms. Pastor John Hagee once said, "God never promised you smooth sailing, but He did promise a safe landing." Nehemiah closed his ears to gossip and criticism, and he opened his heart to God and to his calling to stand in the gap.

STAYING POWER

Sometimes, we stand in the gap for a cause or a person for a short time, and then our role is over. More often, however, God wants us to keep standing in the gap for a long, long time. When Nehemiah finished rebuilding the walls of the city, he could have told people, "Okay, I'm done. I finished what I came here to do, and now I'm going back to my comfortable life in the king's palace in Susa." But Nehemiah didn't say that. He stayed in Jerusalem for twelve years. He knew that opposition hadn't stopped when the last stone was put in place and the last gate was hung. The temptation to compromise, the threats of division, and the storms of his adversaries would continue, so he stayed to protect the walls and care for the people. He wasn't just a builder; he was a believer. He led a reform movement to draw people back to God and to make their faith strong and vibrant. With Ezra, Nehemiah worked hard to restore the city—physically and spiritually.

Quite often, God wants us to build a new culture and a new hope instead of city walls. Martin Luther King, Jr. had the spirit of Nehemiah. He saw the poverty and oppression of African-Americans in the United States and was determined to marshal the power of non-violence to change the nation. He began by leading strikes in Southern cities. However, many in his own community felt uncomfortable with his efforts. Some black leaders advised him to stop because they feared backlash from the white establishment. Again and again, King remained steadfast in the face of opposition—from within his own community and from the entrenched, powerful whites. He was often arrested for speaking out for equality. When he was in the Birmingham jail in 1963, several prominent black clergymen openly questioned his motives and methods. In his famous letter responding to them, he explained,

> "Injustice anywhere is a threat to justice everywhere. We are caught in an inescapable network of mutuality, tied in a single garment of destiny. Whatever affects one directly, affects all indirectly. Never again can we afford to live with the narrow, provincial 'outside agitator' idea. Anyone who lives inside the United States can never be considered an outsider anywhere within its bounds. . . . We know through painful experience that freedom is never voluntarily given by the oppressor; it must be demanded by the oppressed. Frankly, I have yet to engage in a direct action campaign that was 'well-timed' in the

> view of those who have not suffered unduly from the disease of segregation. For years now I have heard the word 'Wait!' It rings in the ear of every Negro with piercing familiarity. This 'Wait' has almost always meant 'Never.' We must come to see, with one of our distinguished jurists, that 'justice too long delayed is justice denied. . . .' So I have tried to make it clear that it is wrong to use immoral means to attain moral ends. But now I must affirm that it is just as wrong, or even more so, to use moral means to preserve immoral ends."[3]

Dr. King's wisdom, courage, and vision were the catalyst that changed a nation—or at least, began to change a nation. He realized staying power was essential. His legacy remains. Leaders today stand on his shoulders to fight for equality and justice.

In many cases, one of our strongest statements of leadership is "just showing up." When Elizabeth and I wanted to build a home, some people advised us to move out to the suburbs and travel back to the city every day. I said, "No, we're going to live in the 'hood. We want to live with our people. We want to share their hopes and their fears." Of course, living in our community isn't as safe as it is out in the suburbs. We've been robbed, and I've even received a death threat. Several times within the first few years of moving into our new home, we were awakened in the middle of the night at the sound of loud blasts from car horns. When we looked out our bedroom window, we could see a car blazing on fire. We soon realized that we had built the house right next to a popular dumpsite for stolen cars. For a moment I feared we had made the wrong choice to move into the neighborhood. The cars were so close to our home—what if one morning we woke and our home was on fire? But then I remembered how important it was that we live in the neighborhood we serve. Our people get robbed and are threatened every day. How can they know we understand them if we don't live in their world? Like Nehemiah, Elizabeth and I want to live, lead, and do life together with the people God has entrusted to our care.

ANOTHER MAN

About 480 years after the walls of Jerusalem were restored, another man rode past the walls of Jerusalem—during the day instead of the night, and on a donkey's colt instead of a horse. A few days later, He fought the world's greatest enemy. In agony, He hung between heaven and earth, between life and death. We were destined for destruction, but Jesus paid the penalty we deserved to pay.

Oh, how those walls could talk! They witnessed the incredible courage of a man who led his people to rebuild and protect them from their enemies, and they watched as another Man gave everything to rescue them from sin and death. Jesus stood in the gap for us. He told the enemy, "You can't take my son! You can't take my daughter! They are mine. I love them so much I'm willing to die to bring them home."

Every time we see Jesus in the Gospels, He's standing in the gap for people. When the religious leaders wanted to stone a woman caught in adultery, Jesus stood between her and her accusers. When blindness or sickness or deformity threatened to ruin a person's life, Jesus stood in the gap to heal. When sin crushed a person's soul, Jesus stood in the gap to offer love and forgiveness. When death took His friend Lazarus, Jesus' heart was broken. He stood in the gap to bring life from the tomb.

Every time we see Jesus in the Gospels, He's standing in the gap for people.

Of course, some don't want Jesus to stand in the gap for them. When Jesus was suspended on the cross between heaven and earth, one thief mocked him, but the other asked Jesus to remember him. That's our choice, too. In fact, when we look at the Gospels, we always see extreme responses to Jesus. No one says, "Oh, He's a nice guy, that's all." They either hate Him, fear Him, or adore Him. When we get even a taste of His grace, He becomes our greatest gift.

Let the love of Jesus move your heart. When that happens, you will see the wonder of His incredible grace, and your heart will break over the empty lives around you. Both—wonder and sorrow—are evidences of a person who finds the courage to identify a problem and dive in to solve it . . . a person like Nehemiah who stands in the gap.

Do you see a problem to solve? Of course you do. Is it your lost child, your angry spouse, your addicted brother or sister, your depressed parent, your annoying neighbor, your demanding co-worker, or something else tugging at your heart? Let compassion fuel your courage to do something about it.

* * * * * * * * * * * *

At the end of each chapter, you'll find a few questions to stimulate reflection and group discussion. It's easy to read a chapter of a book and put it down without wrestling with the principles. Instead, take some time to think, write, and pray over the questions. If you're in a class or small group, use these questions to guide your discussion. I hope your conversations will be rich, and I trust God will use your discussions to build your faith so you'll stand in the gap for those in need around you.

THINK ABOUT IT . . .

1. How would you define and describe what it means to "stand in the gap" for someone?

2. Was weeping a right response to the problem Hanani brought to Nehemiah? Why or why not?

3. Read Nehemiah's prayer in Chapter 1. What stands out to you in the content and zeal of his prayer?

4. When you think of people in need, which of the challenges seems most difficult: compromise, division, or storms? Explain your answer.

5. Why is it important to have staying power as you stand in the gap? What might happen if you were to walk away too soon?

6. What is God saying to you through the story of Nehemiah?

7. What do you hope to get out of this book? How do you want God to work in you and through you as you read it?

2 ESTHER

. . . understood her times

> "Go, gather together all the Jews who are in Susa, and fast for me. Do not eat or drink for three days, night or day. I and my attendants will fast as you do. When this is done, I will go to the king, even though it is against the law. And if I perish, I perish" (Est. 4:16).

I'm fond of the movie character Forrest Gump. One of my favorite scenes is when he sits on a bench next to a quiet woman. He wants to start a conversation, so he offers her chocolates from a box he carries. When she is hesitant to pick one, he speaks a line that has become famous, and one that everyone in my family loves to imitate: "Mama said life was like a box of chocolates. You never know what you're gonna get." We laugh when we try to say it with a Southern accent because we're really bad at it, but we're always reminded of the truth of Forrest's statement.

I believe what Forrest Gump meant is that life is about choices. It's about making the right choice when you're at a crossroads. Choosing the right piece of chocolate isn't as critical as choosing between life and death, but even our simplest choices often surprise us. Esther had that kind of life—a life that caught her by surprise.

In Esther's time the Jewish people were trying to find their place after some major defeats. The Assyrian armies had destroyed the Northern Kingdom, and the Babylonians had conquered the Southern Kingdom. Thousands of Jews had been driven into exile; others remained in their homeland. Slowly, a trickle of refugees began to return home. They first rebuilt the temple in Jerusalem, but the walls had crumbled to dust, leaving the people vulnerable.

For years, God's people lived a fragile existence—those in their devastated homeland as well as the ones still in exile. About thirty years before Nehemiah appeared at the ruined gates of Jerusalem with the king's cavalry and wagonloads of timber, a pivotal event occurred in the Persian king's palace—an event that would determine the fate of the Jewish race. At that moment in history, God used a most unlikely person to stand in the gap to rescue His people.

THE SITUATION

Xerxes (the father of Artaxerxes in Nehemiah's day) was the great king of the Persian Empire, which was centered where Iran is today. Xerxes was his Greek name; his Persian name was Ahasuerus. The story opens with a problem in the king's palace. Vashti, his queen, did something unthinkable: she refused the king's command to attend a major banquet. She may have been having a bad day, but the king was going to make sure she had a *really* bad day! He was so livid that he called all of his advisors to a meeting. The nobles were afraid that other women—their own wives—would be as bold and independent as Vashti. They wanted to quash any hint of Women's Lib, so they gave the king this advice:

> "Therefore, if it pleases the king, let him issue a royal decree and let it be written in the laws of Persia and Media, which cannot be repealed, that Vashti is never again to enter the presence of King Xerxes. Also let the king give her royal position to someone else who is better than she. Then when the king's edict is proclaimed throughout all his vast realm, all the women will respect their husbands, from the least to the greatest" (Est. 1:19–20).

Vashti was banished from the palace forever, so the king needed a new queen. In the custom of ancient Middle Eastern monarchs, Xerxes chose the most beautiful girls in the country for his harem. One was a stunningly beautiful Jewish girl named Hadassah with the Persian name of Esther. She was the younger cousin of a Jewish man named Mordecai. After her parents died, he had raised her as his own daughter.

Biblical names often signify the character and role of the person. In this case, the significance is surprising. The Jewish name, Hadassah, is a myrtle plant. Esther's Persian name means "star," and is probably derived from the Persian goddess Ishtar. So the woman who would play a pivotal role in the history of God's people and the history of redemption had a plain, ordinary spiritual name but a much more impressive foreign name. Her cousin, Mordecai, was named for the pagan god Marduk. Judging from their names alone, no one would have expected God to use them in a significant way. Here's the point: God can use anyone . . . literally anyone.

BUT THERE'S A PROBLEM . . .

For centuries, scholars have observed a distinction in the story of Esther. In other books of the Bible, God shows up in a pillar of fire, a column of smoke, a terrifying earthquake on a mountain, or as a Son of Man who cared for outcasts and died for sinners. But in the book of Esther, God's name is never mentioned. Not even once. We find no miracles, no prayers to God, no pointing to God as the author and sustainer of life.

The problem, however, doesn't stop there. It had been years since the king had decreed that the Jews could return to their homeland, but Mordecai and Esther had apparently decided to stay. They seemingly weren't practicing the Jewish traditions, celebrating Jewish holidays, or following the Jewish laws. Later we discover that Esther didn't even reveal to the king that she was a Jew until she had been queen for four years! In addition, Esther was a member of the king's harem. The Law of Moses expressly forbids illicit sex and mixed marriages.

Esther's story is different from the pure, undefiled life of Daniel and his three friends who had been exiled to Babylon. However, these problems have wonderful, grace-filled answers. God's name may not be mentioned in the account of Esther, but His hand is evident on every page. Behind the scenes, we detect His presence, His power, and His purposes. And we see that God doesn't look for *perfect* people, but *available* people.

God doesn't look for *perfect* people, but *available* people.

The situations in Esther's Persia and our culture today have many similarities. Both are driven by power, pleasure, and possessions, but God is always at work through anyone who is willing to say yes to Him. Esther and Mordecai could have looked at their circumstances and given up in despair. They were exiles, second-class citizens, with no wealth or standing in their society. The God of Abraham, Isaac, and Jacob was ridiculed as impotent or absent. The great kings of Israel, David and Solomon, were mocked. The Word of God was ignored in Persian culture. Esther and Mordecai probably felt cut off from all they held dear and sacred. Who were these two insignificant Jewish people to think they could make a difference?

Today many people in our churches have minds and hearts that are immersed in the pursuit of money, power, excitement, and acclaim. They may go to church every now and then, but they certainly don't have any thought of making a difference for God! Can people like Esther and Mordecai, and people like us, make a difference?

We certainly can! Esther's story can be our story. We can learn from her and her cousin how to stand in the gap in a critical moment in the lives of our family, our neighborhoods, and our culture. God often uses the most unlikely people to accomplish His great purposes. The ancient Persian culture may seem very distant to us, but the truths we find in Esther's story still inspire us today. Paul observed, "For everything that was written in the past was written to teach us, so that through endurance and the encouragement of the Scriptures we might have hope" (Rom. 15:4).

THE CHOICE

In the days of King Xerxes, Internet dating sites hadn't been developed yet—no speed dating, no Facebook, no Instagram. So when the king wanted to find a replacement for Queen Vashti, his personal attendants conducted an extensive search into every corner of the kingdom—not just for one beautiful girl, but for all the ones he might want for his harem. Those gorgeous women would be pampered with beauty treatments for a year, and then "the girl who pleases the king" would become the new queen.

Esther "was lovely in form and features" (Est. 2:7). In other words, she was beautiful! She had the kind of beauty that caused both men and women to turn their heads and stare. After she was selected and made the first cut, she was given special treatment and moved to the "best place in the harem."

For a year, Esther received beauty treatments with special oils, perfumes, and cosmetics. (A year! A lot of guys get upset about their wives or girlfriends taking an extra twenty minutes to get ready!) Every day Mordecai walked outside the palace gates to stay informed about how she was doing. He was worried about her and advised her to remain quiet about her Jewish background.

Finally, the time came for Esther's audition. If the king was pleased with her, she would be invited back. If not, she would vanish into oblivion. She realized her future depended on one man's whim, but she had no idea how much more was at stake.

She passed with flying colors!

> "Now the king was attracted to Esther more than to any of the other women, and she won his favor and approval more than any of the other virgins. So he set a royal crown on her head and made her queen instead of Vashti. And the king gave a great banquet, Esther's banquet, for all his nobles and officials. He proclaimed a holiday throughout the provinces and distributed gifts with royal liberality" (Est. 2:17–18).

During the months before her big audition, can you imagine what must have been going on in the hearts of Esther and Mordecai? Could God possibly smile on her being in the king's harem? What if he didn't like her? Was she right in following Mordecai's advice to keep her ethnicity a secret? Wouldn't it be nobler to be honest from the beginning? And what if the king was irate when he found out, and killed Esther? Her blood might be on Mordecai's hands!

> God is wise, gracious, and powerful enough to weave even our bad choices into something positive and healing.

The main action of the story naturally focuses on Xerxes' choice, but behind the scenes we realize Esther and Mordecai had many fears, doubts, and difficult decisions. Through them all, God was at work in, around, and through two simple people.

The complexity of Esther's situation is a reflection of the real-life circumstances we face, too. Sometimes there are few clear choices—more gray than black and white. Occasionally we feel confused and afraid, and we make some really dumb decisions. But God is wise, gracious, and powerful enough to weave even our bad choices into something positive and healing. We may not get it right, but God does.

No one could rush the king's process. The beautiful, pampered girls may have been impatient to go into the king's chambers, but they needed the year of preparation. In the same way, we often become impatient with our King's process of preparation. In our haste, we see waiting as a waste of time instead of a necessary part of God's equipping us for a special mission. Esther realized she only had one chance to please the king, and she was content to let the process work out.

THE THREAT

After Esther was made queen of Persia, another character—a sinister one—appeared in the drama. Xerxes promoted a man named Haman to the second-highest position in the kingdom, equivalent to the prime minister. Haman was already arrogant, and his new position only made him more imperious. All the other officials knelt to honor him, but Mordecai refused to bow. When the officials told Haman of Mordecai's insubordination, he became enraged. And when he discovered that Mordecai was a Jew, Haman "looked for a way to destroy all Mordecai's people, the Jews, throughout the whole kingdom of Xerxes" (Est. 3:6).

Haman proposed a new royal edict to wipe out the Jewish people in the kingdom. The decree would offer "no quarter," no chance of surrender, no mercy, no toleration. In fact, Haman's hatred of Mordecai and his people was so intense that he offered to pay the king 10,000 talents of silver—about two-thirds of the annual income of the empire—to fund a celebration for getting rid of them. Where would all this money come from? Not from

Haman's pockets. He planned to plunder the Jews he was going to kill.

Soon the royal secretaries were summoned to the palace where they wrote up the decree in the various languages of the kingdom. Xerxes used his ring to mark the decree as his own, and he sent out the death sentence. "Dispatches were sent by couriers to all the king's provinces with the order to destroy, kill and annihilate all the Jews—young and old, women and little children—on a single day, the thirteenth day of the twelfth month, the month of Adar, and to plunder their goods" (Est. 3:13).

At the time, over nine million Jews lived in the Persian Empire. When the decree was issued, they were all living on borrowed time.

THE COURAGE OF ONE

Esther was completely unaware of Haman's evil plans. She was a queen, not a politician. But Mordecai lived in the streets of Susa. When he learned of the decree, he followed the traditions of anguished grief by tearing his clothes and putting on sack-cloth and ashes. He wasn't alone. Jews all over the realm knew their end was fast approaching.

Esther's maids told her about Mordecai's despair, and she was deeply distressed. She sent him some new clothes to replace the torn ones, but he refused to wear them. What good were new clothes when he was going to be murdered?

Quite often we try to minimize the horror of danger—to ourselves or others—by distracting our minds with entertainment or numbing our hearts with possessions or pursuits. In the palace, the king tried to solve every problem by buying people off with titles or giving them lavish gifts. Esther was living in splendor and thought she could soothe Mordecai's anguish with some new clothes, but he knew the danger was real.

Mordecai realized there was only one person who had the king's ear and could stop the annihilation of the Jews. He sent word to Esther to go to the king to beg for mercy—for herself and all of her people.

Esther had everything to lose. She was the queen of the most powerful nation on earth. She had unimaginable wealth and prestige. She was the envy of every woman and the secret desire of every man in the land. And surely she had a severely conflicted identity: Was she Jewish or pagan? Was her name Hadassah or Esther? Did she belong in the palace with Xerxes or with her cousin and her people? Was she loyal to God or to the Persian king? Were the perfumes, oils, beautiful clothes, delicious food, and prestige of being queen more important than the plight of her people?

Yet Mordecai's plea cut through Esther's heart like a knife. When she considered the implications of Mordecai's request, she shuddered. She sent back a chilling message:

> "All the king's officials and the people of the royal provinces know that for any man or woman who approaches the king in the inner court without being summoned the king has but one law: that they be put to death unless the king extends the gold scepter to them and spares their lives. But thirty days have passed since I was called to go to the king" (Est. 4:11).

In Persia and much of the ancient world, husbands ruled. Xerxes had a law that his wives, even the queen, couldn't approach him in his man cave unless he specifically invited them. (Some husbands today would like to reintroduce this law in their homes, especially when they're watching a game on television.)

Mordecai realized Esther needed some steel in her backbone. She may have thought she could hide in the palace while other Jews were slaughtered. She may have wondered if anything so cruel would really be carried out. The enormity of the crime was simply too much to fathom. Mordecai was asking Esther to risk her position, her wealth, her comfort, and her life for her people.

Many centuries later, the Jews again faced total destruction. And again, the threat seemed too horrible, too evil, too egregious to believe. In his book, *Night,* Elie Wiesel describes the unbelief of the Jewish leaders in his town in Hungary when they first heard the Nazis' plans to annihilate them. A young man named Moishe Beadle had been taken from the town and shipped off for "relocation." A few months later, Moishe returned with wild eyes, a frantic voice, and a stern warning. Wiesel writes:

> "He told me what had happened to him and his companions. The train with the deportees had crossed the Hungarian border and, once in Polish territory, had been taken over by the Gestapo. The train had stopped. The Jews were ordered to get off and onto waiting trucks. The trucks headed toward a forest. There everybody was ordered to get out. They were forced to dig huge trenches. When they had finished their work, the men from the Gestapo began theirs. Without passion or haste, they shot their prisoners, who were forced to approach the trench line one by one and offer their necks. Infants were tossed into the air and used as targets for the machine guns."

Wiesel asked Moishe how he had escaped. He explained that he had been shot in the leg and left for dead. The people in the town, though, just shook their heads when Moishe begged them to run for their lives. Some suggested he wanted to be the center of attention. Others said he was insane.

No one took him seriously. Who could believe the story could possibly be true? After days and weeks of trying to persuade people, Moishe finally gave up. "You don't understand," he said in despair. "You cannot understand. I was saved miraculously. I succeeded in coming back. Where did I get my strength? I wanted to return to [the town] to describe to you my death so that you might ready yourselves while there is still time. Life? I no longer care to live. I am alone. But I wanted to come back to warn you. Only no one is listening to me. . . ."[4]

Mordecai was like Moishe. He hoped that a single person would listen to him and take action. With all the urgency he could summon, he sent this word to Esther:

> "Do not think that because you are in the king's house you alone of all the Jews will escape. For if you remain silent at this time, relief and deliverance for the Jews will arise from another place, but you and your father's family will perish. And who knows but that you have come to your royal position for such a time as this?" (Est. 4:13–14)

Esther was at a crossroads . . . a big one. She was standing at the dividing point of history—for herself, for her cousin, and for the nine million Jews in Persia. Until that moment, her ethnicity and faith had been secret. Until that moment, she had been living in luxury in a pagan king's palace. Until that moment, her beauty had carried her through. Until that moment, she had been passive, waited on hand and foot. But in that moment everything changed. Mordecai's message was simple, but it called her to make a choice: "If you go to the king without being summoned, you *might* die. If you don't go, you, I, and every other Jew in the kingdom *certainly will* die. It's your choice."

We can wander in a wealthy world thinking only about the next phone upgrade, the next great restaurant, the next vacation, or the next promotion. But sometimes God breaks through our complacency to show us a purpose far bigger than ourselves. When God shows us a crying need and puts it on our hearts, He is giving us something to live for. Suddenly, for Esther, the years of pampering made perfect sense. God had put her in the role of queen to stand in the gap for her persecuted people. Up to that point, other people had been making decisions for Esther, but it was time for her to take charge. Her first bold action was to ask for prayer. She sent instructions to Mordecai. Note the beautiful blend of dependence on God and steely resolve:

When God shows us a crying need and puts it on our hearts, He is giving us something to live for.

> "Go, gather together all the Jews who are in Susa, and fast for me. Do not eat or drink for three days, night or day. I and my attendants will fast as you do. When this is done, I will go to the king, even though it is against the law. And if I perish, I perish" (Est. 4:16).

The narrative doesn't tell us that God wrote on a wall, spoke in a whirlwind, or appeared in a burning bush. God's people prayed for Esther, but she didn't demand a sign. She simply said, "You pray. I'll go. And we'll leave the results in God's hands."

Sometimes God graciously gives us a prophetic word or a vision of the future, but more often, we're like Esther: we know the right thing to do, and we do it without knowing how it will turn out.

For three days and nights, God's people prayed. And for three days and nights, Esther prepared herself for one bold act of outrageous courage. On the third day, she put on her robes and stood in the king's hall of the palace. When the king saw her, he held out his gold scepter and invited her to come in. Obviously, this was no social visit.

Xerxes said, "What is it, Queen Esther? What is your request? Even up to half the kingdom, it will be given you" (Est. 5:3).

I don't know if Esther almost fainted. I think I would have. She had been looking into the face of death . . . and the king smiled. A reprieve! But her work was not yet done. First she asked him only to attend a banquet with a limited invitation list: just the king, Esther, and Haman.

At the banquet, the king asked her to share her request. As the coy hostess of this intimate banquet, Esther asked the king and Haman to return the next day for another banquet. She promised to tell him her request at that time.

Haman was very happy all that afternoon. He had recently been promoted to the second position of power in the kingdom, and he had gotten the decree passed to kill all the Jews. That day the queen had honored him at a feast for the royal couple, and he was invited back the next day, too! He was riding high!

But as he walked out of the palace, he saw Mordecai. Everyone else bowed to Haman, but not Mordecai. When Haman got home, he complained to his friends and his wife how that Jew had dishonored him—an insult especially despicable in light of the honor shown him by the queen. He said, "I should be really happy, but I'm miserable—because Mordecai still lives!"

His wife had a solution: "Have a pole set up, reaching to a height of fifty cubits, and ask the king in the morning to have Mordecai impaled on it. Then go with the king to the banquet and enjoy yourself" (Est. 5:14). Haman loved the idea. He ordered the gallows built at once.

PROVIDENCE

We have seen that in the book of Esther the name of God is never mentioned—there are no prayers and no miracles, but God wasn't absent. We can see His fingerprints clearly in His providential care and direction. God's providence can be defined this way: "God, in some invisible and mysterious way, governs all creatures, actions, and circumstances through the normal and ordinary course of human life, without the intervention of the miraculous."[5]

At this point in the story, God's providence shows up in a big way! The same night the gallows were being constructed, the king couldn't sleep. He asked for the official history of his reign to be brought in and read to him. Maybe he thought it would be so boring it would put him to sleep, but it had the opposite effect. The account read to him was about Mordecai, who once had exposed an assassination attempt on the king's life (Est. 2:21–23; 6:1–3).

The king asked the reader, "What honor and recognition has Mordecai received for this?"

He was told, "Nothing has been done for him."

Xerxes asked, "Who is in the court?"

At that precise moment Haman had just walked in, planning to tell the king about the gallows and his plans to execute Mordecai the next day. When the attendant announced that Haman was in the court, Xerxes invited him to come into his bedchamber. The king asked Haman, "What should be done for the man the king delights to honor?" (Est. 6:3–6)

Can you see the delight on Haman's face? Can you feel his pride and joy? He assumes the king is talking about him! He couldn't wait to answer:

> "For the man the king delights to honor, have them bring a royal robe the king has worn and a horse the king has ridden, one with a royal crest placed on its head. Then let the robe and horse be entrusted to one of the king's most noble princes. Let them robe the man the king delights to honor, and lead him on the horse through the city streets, proclaiming before him, 'This is what is done for the man the king delights to honor!'" (Est. 6:7–9)

The king loved Haman's idea! He told him, "Go at once." I'm sure Haman was so excited . . . until the king dropped the hammer: "Get the robe and the horse and do just as you have suggested for Mordecai the Jew, who sits at the king's gate. Do not neglect anything you have recommended" (Est. 6:10).

The narrative doesn't record Haman's reaction at that moment, but it doesn't take much to imagine what he wanted to say: *Mordecai! You've got to be kidding! I guess this isn't the right time to ask if I have permission to hang him tomorrow, huh?*

The next day, with sweet irony, Haman grudgingly led his archenemy, Mordecai, around the city on the king's horse and wearing the king's royal robe. It almost killed Haman every time he announced, "This is what is done for the man the king delights to honor!" (Est. 6:11)

As soon as the parade was finished, it was time for Haman to hurry to the second banquet with the king and queen. Again, the king asked Esther to tell him her request, and again, he promised to fulfill it.

This time she was forthcoming. She asked him to spare her people, who had been "sold to be destroyed, killed and annihilated" (Est. 7:3–4). She explained that if the decree had only made them slaves, she wouldn't even have bothered the king, but the extermination of an entire people was too severe.

The king was shocked and outraged. He asked her, "Who is he? Where is the man who has dared to do such a thing?"

She replied, "An adversary and enemy! This vile Haman!"

The king was infuriated and left the room as Haman remained to beg Esther for mercy. When the king returned, Haman had thrown himself on the couch where Esther was reclining. The king shouted, "Will he even molest the queen while she is with me in the house?"

One of the attendants had a solution. He told Xerxes, "A gallows seventy-five feet high stands by Haman's house. He had it made for Mordecai, who spoke up to help the king."

The king instantly proclaimed, "Hang him on it!" They took Haman out to the gallows he had constructed, and there he died (Est. 7:3–10).

The problem facing the Jews, though, wasn't resolved by Haman's death. The edict still stood because the law of the Medes and Persians was irrevocable. What could be done? Esther and Mordecai asked the king to issue another decree to overrule the first one. Xerxes was glad to send out a second edict giving the Jews the right to protect themselves and to plunder the property of anyone who attacked them.

The salvation of the Jewish people in Persia is celebrated in the Feast of Purim. The first feast day took place when the couriers went out to every corner of the empire:

"The city of Susa held a joyous celebration. For the Jews it was a time of happiness and joy, gladness and honor. In every province and in every city to which the edict of the king came, there was joy and gladness among the Jews, with feasting and celebrating. And many people of other nationalities became Jews because fear of the Jews had seized them" (Est. 8:15–17).

ESTHER UNDERSTOOD HER TIMES

A crisis can confuse us, or it can clear away the cobwebs and enable us to think more clearly. Esther had lived a double life. She had a background of faith, but she found herself in a pagan world. In fact, she reached the top of her pagan world as queen of the land. She had it all—staggering wealth and sublime beauty—so she had everything to lose. The plight of her people, though, shattered her illusions. She realized she could no longer live simply for herself.

A crisis can confuse us, or it can clear away the cobwebs and enable us to think more clearly.

She realized the risks. She told Mordecai, "If I perish, I perish." She was willing to lay it all on the line for her people, no matter what the cost. This was her time, her moment, her task, her God-given purpose. She may previously have had selfish desires, but now she had only one: to rescue her people. Centuries later, James, Jesus' half-brother, warned about having a divided mind and heart:

> "If any of you lacks wisdom, you should ask God, who gives generously to all without finding fault, and it will be given to you. But when you ask, you must believe and

> not doubt, because the one who doubts is like a wave of the sea, blown and tossed by the wind. That person should not expect to receive anything from the Lord. Such a person is double-minded and unstable in all they do" (James 1:5–8).

We might say, "Well, that was then, this is now. We don't live in ancient Persia or first-century Palestine. We don't have a king. Things are different." Yes, things on the surface are very different, but underneath, human nature hasn't changed at all. People are just as selfish, just as divided in their loyalties, just as evil, and just as victimized as they were twenty or twenty-five centuries ago. People in trouble need someone like Mordecai to be touched deeply, to weep and grieve, and to enlist the help of those in a position to help. And people in trouble need someone like Esther, who may have been oblivious until realizing the need for courage to take bold action at "such a time as this."

Dietrich Bonhoeffer understood his times. In the early 1930s, most Germans, including pastors, believed Adolph Hitler was engineering a miraculous recovery of their devastated economy and national identity. Bonhoeffer quickly comprehended the threat of this evil man and his aims. Only two days after Hitler became Chancellor of the nation, Bonhoeffer gave a radio address warning his countrymen. As Hitler accrued more power and silenced opposition, Bonhoeffer's prophetic voice became even louder and clearer. Late in the '30s, he sailed to America where he hoped to teach at a seminary. His heart, though, was with his people, and he determined to return to his homeland. He explained to a close friend,

> "I have come to the conclusion that I made a mistake in coming to America. I must live through this difficult period in our national history with the people of Germany. I will have no right to participate in the reconstruction of Christian life in Germany after the war if I do not share the trials of this time with my people. . . . Christians in Germany will have to face the terrible alternative of either willing the defeat of their nation in order that Christian civilization may survive or willing the victory of their nation and thereby destroying civilization. I know which of these alternatives I must choose but I cannot make that choice from security."[6]

Bonhoeffer didn't have the luxury of making his difficult choice from a position of security. Most people insist on feeling secure before they make hard decisions. They know the right choices but fail to act because they don't feel completely comfortable. For Bonhoeffer and other courageous people, a sense of urgency propels them to bold action. In a daring move,

For Bonhoeffer and other courageous people, a sense of urgency propels them to bold action.

Bonhoeffer joined the German underground resistance movement. The noble pastor was implicated in a plot to assassinate the Fuhrer and was arrested in April, 1943. Two years later, with the end of the war only weeks away, he was executed. A Nazi doctor who witnessed his last moments wrote, "I saw Pastor Bonhoeffer . . . kneeling on the floor praying fervently to God. I was most deeply moved by the way this lovable man prayed, so devout and so certain that God heard his prayer. At the place of execution, he again said a short prayer and then climbed the few steps to the gallows, brave and composed. His death ensued after a few seconds. In the almost fifty years that I worked as a doctor, I have hardly ever seen a man die so entirely submissive to the will of God."[7]

Like Esther, Bonhoeffer recognized the urgency of his times. He was not willing to surrender to the forces of darkness in his world. In his work, *Ethics,* he commented, "There is not a place to which the Christian can withdraw from the world, whether it be outwardly or in the sphere of the inner life. Any attempt to escape from the world must sooner or later be paid for with a sinful surrender to the world."[8]

The story of Esther should encourage us deeply. God didn't use someone who had a great background, had lived a pure life, and always faithfully obeyed Him. God used someone who was deeply flawed, had divided priorities, and was not even aware of the problem until someone told her about it. Do you fit this description? We all do.

All of us have defining moments. Sometimes they come and go in an instant, so we must be ready. More often, we have more time—either to respond with wisdom and courage, or to make excuses and walk away.

A single mother in our community realized her children were being exposed to values in their school that threatened all she wanted to impart to them. Her kids were coming home asking about same-sex marriage because they had heard their teacher talk about "Bob and Paul forming a family." She explained the situation and asked for my advice. I'm an activist, so I encouraged her to get involved. She became a member of the school council, and in that role she has made a difference. She has successfully changed some of the most offensive curriculum, but not by being angry and demanding. With a beautiful blend of diplomacy, kindness, and courage she has helped create a culture of strong values and genuine peace in her kids' school.

Look around. Do you see people in trouble? Are men and women, boys and girls threatened with destruction? Sometimes they're the victims of others' sins; sometimes they are suffering from their own foolish, selfish choices. Either way, they're slipping away into the abyss. Do you notice? Do you care? Of course you do, or you wouldn't be reading this book!

You stand at a crossroad—between someone in desperate need and God's desire to use you. The situation, the timing, and the opportunity didn't happen by chance. You're there by the providence of God . . . for such a time as this. You have an incredible opportunity. No more excuses. No more blaming others for not doing enough about the problem. No more minimizing the difficulty by saying, "Oh, it's not that bad." No more denial that the problem even exists.

Esther had been passive for a long time, but when the defining moment came, she acted. Ask God to awaken your heart and give you Esther's courage. Ask Him to give you compassion and wisdom like Mordecai. You can make a difference. This is your time.

The king asked Esther two questions, "What is your petition? What is your request?" To parallel questions, Esther gave parallel answers: "Grant me my life—this is my petition, and spare my people—this is my request." By answering in such a way, she was saying that her life and the lives of her people were one. She identified with her people. She may have been double-minded before, but no longer. Their fate was her fate.

We should make the same request as we stand in the gap for those around us. But the King who hears our request is far greater than Xerxes. Because Esther identified with the fate of God's people, she shared in the destiny of God's people. God used this woman—this deeply flawed and previously double-minded woman—to change the course of history.

Often we assume nothing we do really matters in the grand scheme of things. We don't see our lives making a dent in the enormous problems of the world. Thankfully, Mordecai and

Esther didn't see it that way (at least after they became aware of the threat). Each person's contribution matters. Every act of love counts. Every courageous deed makes a difference.

When we read the story of Esther, we realize it's a pivotal moment in the long story of the gospel of grace, from Abraham to Moses to David to Esther, and from there to Christ, to Paul, and to every congregation of believers today. If Haman had succeeded in his plot to exterminate the Jews, God's work would have come to an end. There would have been no Jewish people, no Christ, no church, and no hope for you and me. But in the sovereignty, wisdom, and grace of Almighty God, He used two people to maintain the course of history and fulfill His will.

Each person's contribution matters. Every act of love counts. Every courageous deed makes a difference.

The account of Esther isn't an obscure story about ancient history. It's an important part of your story and mine. The courage of Esther and Mordecai led to Jesus' coming, dying, and giving us new life. Because Esther identified with God's people, she opened the door to the destiny of God's future people—you and me. God's name may not be mentioned in this story, but we see His providential care in every line. No power, even the king's edict, could stand against God's purposes and plans for His people—then or now.

In Esther's story, we get to look behind the scenes to see God at work when no one could see His hand. Even in their darkest night and fiercest threat, God was providentially weaving the strands of history into a beautiful story of redemption. In Esther, and in our own lives, we affirm that Paul was right: "We know that in all things God works for the good of those who love him, who have been called according to his purpose" (Rom. 8:28).

What request do you bring before the King? He's summoning you now. Go to Him. Be brave. This is your time.

THINK ABOUT IT . . .

1. Are beauty (or being handsome) and wealth a blessing or a curse? Explain your answer.

2. What does it mean to have "a divided heart"? Describe the division in Esther's life. What were its causes, and what were the dangers?

3. What are some examples of "pivotal moments" in a marriage . . . in a family . . . in a community . . . and in a nation? What are reasons some people rise to seize that moment, and what are some reasons others make excuses and walk away? What is your request of the King?

4. What risk did Esther take? Can you relate to her situation in any way? What are the risks for you if you realize it's your time to act with outrageous courage?

5. In what way is Esther the hero of this story? In what way is Mordecai the hero?

6. How would you define and describe God's providence to a friend who isn't familiar with the Bible? What is the most striking evidence of God working behind the scenes in this story? (You have plenty of options!)

7. What is God saying to you through the story of Esther?

3 NOAH

. . . was "all in," no matter what the cost

"So the LORD said, 'I will wipe from the face of the earth the human race I have created—and with them the animals, the birds and the creatures that move along the ground—for I regret that I have made them.' But Noah found favor in the eyes of the LORD" (Gen. 6:7–8).

The city of New Orleans was founded in 1718. Only four years later, a hurricane destroyed it. The governor of Louisiana warned the people that the city was built too low—parts of it were below sea level—but they chose to remain there anyway. Almost three centuries later, in 2000, the Army Corps of Engineers recommended strengthening the city dikes. They estimated the cost would be about $30 million. However, the officials decided it was too expensive. Five years later, Hurricane Katrina slammed into the Louisiana coast, bursting the dikes, flooding much of New Orleans, and killing 1,833 people. The cost to rebuild the devastated city was $81 billion. Warnings often sound foolish, ridiculous, silly . . . before a disaster strikes.

Today the news is filled with warnings, if we will only listen:

- In the richest nation the world has ever seen, one in six Americans lives in poverty.[9]
- States report that from 14 percent to 32 percent of adults engage in binge drinking.[10]
- The average age a woman becomes a prostitute is fourteen. Ninety-two percent of prostitutes say they can't leave the lifestyle because they lack money and food.[11]
- According to the FBI, America has 33,000 violent street, motorcycle, or prison gangs, with a combined total of more than 1.4 million members.[12]
- Many states are passing laws to permit same-sex marriage and marijuana use.
- About half of the world's population lives on less than $2.50 a day.[13]
- In the world today, there are between 20 and 30 million slaves. Some are forced into child labor, but most are sex slaves.[14]
- Rogue nations have already developed or are trying to develop nuclear weapons. The leaders of those nations threaten to use them, and they don't seem to be bluffing.

THEN AND NOW

When we compare current news reports to the conditions when Noah and his family lived, we might conclude not much has changed. In the generations following Adam's and Eve's expulsion from the Garden of Eden, human beings didn't exactly shine like lights on a hill! In a chilling description of a broken, wicked culture, the Bible says: "The LORD saw how great the wickedness of the human race had become on the earth, and that every inclination of the thoughts of the human heart was only evil all the time. . . . Now the earth was corrupt in God's sight and was full of violence. God saw how corrupt the earth had become, for all the people on earth had corrupted their ways" (Gen. 6:5, 11–12).

Evil doesn't start with actions; it begins with selfish, twisted thoughts.

The problem wasn't isolated or limited. This is a shocking indictment: "every inclination of the thoughts of the human heart was only evil all the time." The entire human race was corrupt in "their ways," which includes twisted purposes, abusive relationships, vile words, and darkened hearts. Evil doesn't start with actions; it begins with selfish, twisted thoughts. A sin is conceived in the mind, considered in the heart, and then pursued with action (James 1:13–15). It may take only an instant for a secret temptation to become a visible sin, or we may plot and plan it for a long time.

In his letter to the Romans, Paul contrasted the outcomes of evil thoughts and holy thoughts:

> "Those who live according to the flesh have their minds set on what the flesh desires; but those who live in accordance with the Spirit have their minds set on what the Spirit desires. The mind governed by the flesh is death, but the mind governed by the Spirit is life and peace. The mind governed by the flesh is hostile to God; it does not submit to God's law, nor can it do so. Those who are in the realm of the flesh cannot please God" (Rom. 8:5–8).

Of course, even wicked people believe they're doing the right things for the right reasons. A murderer claims his victim "deserved it." A rapist insists his victim "wanted it." A liar shrugs, "It worked out better this way." People have an almost unlimited capacity for self-deception and blame-shifting.

In response to the rampant wickedness, God's heart was deeply grieved. We may suppose He was furious, but the writer of Genesis (we assume it was Moses) described God's response to the sin of that day like Jesus when He wept at the tomb of Lazarus—His heart was broken. Some of us think God delights in blasting people who stray from Him, but that couldn't be more wrong. God only delights in showering people with love and blessing, and He loves it when we respond with grateful hearts. He is exceedingly patient, like the parent of a toddler who falls as many times as he stands. Jesus wept at the tomb of Lazarus and as He walked into Jerusalem realizing the people there would reject His gracious offer of forgiveness. God weeps at the beginning of Noah's story because those He created, those He loved, those He longed to bless had turned their backs on Him.

When God spoke to Moses, He identified himself as, "The LORD, the LORD, the compassionate and gracious God, slow to anger, abounding in love and faithfulness" (Ex. 34:6). *Slow to anger and abounding in love.* That's the God we know, love, and serve.

Many years later, Jesus referred to Noah in regard to His coming back to earth in His glory: "As it was in the days of Noah, so it will be at the coming of the Son of Man" (Matt. 24:37). So as we read the account of Noah and the cleansing flood, we shouldn't relegate it to the level of fairy tales. It's a historical account of fallen, corrupt, wicked human life. It addresses a problem that still exists today and will continue until the trumpet sounds and Jesus returns in bodily form to the earth to set up His eternal kingdom.

What were the conditions when this account began? We read about an exploding population, sexual perversion, demonic activity, evil motives, cultural corruption, and violence. We see similar conditions today: a population of almost seven billion people; an epidemic of pornography and graphic sex in the media; widespread adultery; a fascination with zombies and demons; children abusing other kids so horribly that they commit suicide; and persistent problems with drugs, violence, gangs, rape, and murder.

At creation, God had repeatedly celebrated, "It is good." By Noah's day He had to say, "This is not good—not good at all." He had rejoiced in creation, and He would grieve over its destruction.

When a society experiences moral failure, God looks for a man or a woman to stand in the gap—someone who will have hope when everything seems hopeless, to have faith when the situation is dark and dire, and to lead when almost no one will follow. God found Noah.

WHY NOAH?

We have seen that a gap is a place of weakness, vulnerability, and danger. It's a place where desperate needs are exposed, where people are threatened. If a gap is a place where integrity is compromised and God's standards have been shattered, Noah was standing in one of the biggest, most dangerous gaps in all of history! Noah shows us that it's possible to be godly in a godless generation.

Most of the gaps we face are in our own lives or in our families. We may struggle with habitual sin we can't seem to shake.

Finances, health, or careers are in shambles. A marriage hits a rocky place, or maybe it's disintegrating before our eyes. A child has walked away from us and from God. A parent can no longer care for herself. These are the most common gaps in our lives. But if we use a wider lens, we see far bigger, society-wide threats. Those not only are dangerous for a person or a family; they can swamp an entire culture. That was the kind Noah faced.

Standing in a gap is costly. It requires a sacrifice of our time, our energy, and our hearts.

Standing in a gap is costly. It requires a sacrifice of our time, our energy, and our hearts. We can expect opposition, ridicule, and mocking from others—even those we thought would support us and appreciate our efforts. Noah had no idea how much he would have to sacrifice when he said yes to God. It didn't matter. He was "all in."

Only two people in the Old Testament are said to have expressly "found favor in the eyes of God": Noah and Moses. Both rescued God's people from annihilation—one from God's judgment of wickedness, the other from God's judgment on Pharaoh, sin, and death. Noah built an ark to save people and animals; Moses gave instructions to kill an animal to save his people. Noah would sail over a destroying flood; Moses pointed to the blood of a lamb to protect people from the Destroyer, the Angel of Death. The Bible tells us about three arks: Noah's huge ship, the basket Moses' mother put him in so he could float in the Nile River and be found by Pharaoh's daughter, and the ark of the covenant containing the Ten Commandments, a jar of manna, and Aaron's rod. All of them protect; all of them point to God's salvation; all of them speak of His grace.

A lot of people get mixed up when they read the Bible. They think they see two different Gods: a mean God of the Old Testament, and a nice God (Jesus) in the New Testament. I have to conclude that such people haven't read much of the Bible because the story of God's grace and redemption are on every page, from first to last. The message of Scripture does not break cleanly into two parts: law in the Old Testament and grace in the New. Rather, the Bible covers four themes: creation, fall, redemption, and restoration. Creation and the fall of the human race into sin are recounted in the first three chapters of Genesis. The ultimate restoration of the garden—the New Heaven and New Earth—is described at the end of Revelation (and a few other scattered passages). Everything in between is about God's grace and redemption!

I offer this explanation so people won't assume Noah found favor in God's eyes because he followed the rules well enough to impress God. It is, has always been, and always will be faith in God's redeeming grace that saves people and puts us in the family of God. "Abraham believed God, and it was credited to him as righteousness" (Gen. 15:6; Rom. 4:3). And the writer to the Hebrews reminds us, "Without faith it is impossible to please God" (Heb. 11:6).

The word *favor* means "grace." Noah found God's grace, or more accurately, God's grace found Noah. God's favor is unmerited; it can never be earned. We can never do enough to impress God. Those who come to God must be "poor in spirit," realizing they are spiritually bankrupt and empty apart from God. We humbly admit we are so flawed it took the death of the Son of God to pay for our sins, but He loves us so much He was glad to do it.

In the Old Testament, the animal sacrifices were symbols of the ultimate future sacrifice. The unblemished lambs on the altar pointed to "the Lamb of God who takes away the sin of the world." God's offer has been the same for Noah, Abraham, Moses, David, Paul, Peter, and your Aunt Maria: "Trust in My sacrifice for your sins, and become My beloved child by faith."

Noah was a rare example in his day because he accepted the grace of God. He was unlike all the people around him. They delighted in evil; he delighted in God. Their purpose was to get all they could get any way they could get it; Noah's purpose was to please the One who offered him amazing grace.

In the Sermon on the Mount, Jesus contrasts two roads, two gates, two trees, and two houses. Many people assume He was talking about good people and bad people. He was not. He was describing two sets of people who are both doing right things, but for entirely different reasons. Some folks do right things as leverage to get God to love and accept them (and probably to impress those around them). Others do right things simply out of joyful gratitude for the grace of God poured out to them. Same activities, but very different motives.

Noah's obedience was a response to God's grace. When the redeeming love of God fills our hearts, we find incredible courage.

- We can be obedient to God even when we're surrounded by selfish, rebellious people.
- We don't play games with God; we're transformed by His grace.
- We can demonstrate great faith even though others are filled with fear.
- We choose to follow God's directions instead of living by erratic feelings.
- We are willing to be "all in" with God's purposes when everyone around us is screaming, "Look out for number one!"

God had been extremely patient with the wicked people of Noah's time. Even though His heart was broken because they turned their backs on Him, He said, "My Spirit will not contend with humans forever, for they are mortal; their days will be a hundred and twenty years" (Gen. 6:3). He gave them 120 years to repent and turn back to Him.

During that time, God gave Noah and his sons (Shem, Ham, and Japheth) instructions to build a huge boat, and it took them that long to construct it. You can imagine the scorn and mocking they suffered from people who watched them labor day after day.

Noah didn't suffer quietly; he preached to the sinners (2 Pet. 2:5). I don't know if his sons and their wives sang in the choir before his message, and I somehow doubt they passed the offering plate. Yet for 120 years, Noah preached the same sermon: "You've broken God's heart, but He loves you. Turn back to Him." It appears that no one listened. When the doors of the ark closed, only Noah and his family were on board. If I had been Noah, I would have been pretty discouraged, but Noah's faith was strong. He and his sons kept working, kept building, kept trusting, and kept waiting for the rain to fall. They knew it was coming, and they would be ready.

The Bible says, "Noah was a righteous man, blameless among the people of his time, and he walked faithfully with God" (Gen. 6:9). Let's look at those characteristics.

Noah was righteous.

This is the first time the word *righteous* is found in the Bible. It can be used in two different ways: as a position before God, and to describe behavior. Human beings are inherently sinful, separated from God. How can we possibly be considered righteous? Only as a gift of grace. We confess that we're sinners in need of a Savior.

In response, God forgives us and cleanses us from all unrighteousness (1 John 1:9), and then He goes a step farther. He clothes us in Christ's own righteousness. When the Father looks at us, He sees us wrapped in the righteousness of Jesus Christ.

Paul explained the greatest swap in history: "God made [Christ] who had no sin to be sin for us, so that in him we might become the righteousness of God" (2 Cor. 5:21). On the cross, Jesus bore all our sins and died in our place. He took the punishment we deserved. When we trust in Him, Christ's righteousness is credited to our account. Amazing.

The more our hearts are melted by the wonderful love of God and molded to be a little more like Him, the more our actions change. We increasingly want what God wants, we care about the things He cares about, and we give, love, and serve the way Jesus did. Our new position then transforms our behavior: prompted by grace, our actions become more righteous.

How did Noah obey, remain strong, and speak out for God in a perverse generation? Only because he had experienced the swap: his sins for God's righteousness.

Noah was blameless.

Righteousness describes Noah's position before God; blamelessness describes his conduct around people. It doesn't mean he was sinless. Only one person has ever fit that description. But Noah had integrity: his words matched his actions.

Noah was faithful.

Before translating the version of the Bible known as *The Message*, Eugene Peterson wrote a book called *A Long Obedience in the Same Direction: Discipleship in an Instant Society*. The theme of the book is important: It's one thing to be obedient to God for a short time; it's entirely something else to be faithful over the long haul, through valleys and over mountains, in good times and bad, when we see God's hand clearly and when it seems He's a million miles away. During Noah's 120 years of hard work, rainless skies, and constant heckling, he demonstrated amazing faithfulness. His life was a long obedience in the same direction.

It's one thing to be obedient to God for a short time; it's entirely something else to be faithful over the long haul, through valleys and over mountains, in good times and bad, when we see God's hand clearly and when it seems He's a million miles away.

Most of us have a hard time being faithful to God's calling for more than a week or two, especially if we face opposition and seemingly unreasonable delays. Noah kept going for 120 years! And based on the account in Genesis, God only spoke to him one time. Many people feel insecure about God's leading and want Him to repeat His assurances over and over again. Noah may have desired that as well, but he didn't require it. God spoke once. That was enough for him.

At the end of the construction project, the Bible gives Noah a performance review: "Noah did everything just as God commanded him" (Gen. 6:22). Wow! Many years later, Jesus told a parable about three servants. Two of them heard a report much like Noah's: "Well done, good and faithful servant! You have been faithful with a few things; I will put you in charge of many things. Come and share your master's happiness!" (Matt. 25:21)

Was Noah's faithfulness important? I'll say it was! If Noah had given up or bailed out on God, no one would have survived. Abraham wouldn't have received the promise, Moses wouldn't have been born, David wouldn't have been a king, and we wouldn't exist. Your DNA and mine go back to Noah and his family. One man's faithfulness and obedience to God was crucial in the history of the planet. Noah stood in the gap for us all. One man's obedience shaped our destiny. The writer to the Hebrews tells us, "By faith Noah, when warned about things not yet seen, in holy fear built an ark to save his family. By his faith he condemned the world and became heir of the righteousness that is in keeping with faith" (Heb. 11:7).

Noah built a ship on dry ground. To others, his actions appeared foolish, but it was an act of authentic faith in God and His command. His faith was combined with "holy fear." He had the right kind of fear—fear of God, not fear of what people would think of him. This is the kind of reverence we would feel if we were to meet the President or the Queen of England. Noah believed God is majestic, all-powerful, all-knowing, wise, loving, and strong beyond all comprehension. God isn't our butler or waiter. He isn't our "good buddy" or Santa Claus. We don't do deals with the awesome God of creation who spoke and flung the stars into space! No, we humbly fall at His feet, thank Him for His grace, and offer ourselves to Him in glad obedience. That's what He deserves.

God is far more concerned about our character than our reputation. If we're smart, we'll have the same priority.

Before Noah built the ark, God built Noah's faith and character. God doesn't entrust mighty endeavors to people who don't believe He is worthy of their love and loyalty. *Character* is who you are when no one is looking. *Reputation* is people's perception of your character. God is far more concerned about our character than our reputation. If we're smart, we'll have the same priority.

We can easily imagine the temptation for Noah and his sons to give in to criticism and bail out on God's command. Noah's three sons were young boys at the beginning of this process. One of them could have said, "Hey, Dad. We want to stop working now. We're going to a party, okay?"

Noah would have replied, "Son, don't lose focus. This is important. In fact, the future of the world depends on us."

And Noah's neighbors probably walked past him every day mocking and jeering, "Hey Noah, any rain today? No, I haven't felt any either. You're a moron. You're wasting your life, man. Come on, stop building that stupid thing and get a real job!"

After twenty years, did Noah and his sons have second thoughts? After forty or fifty years of sweat and toil—and no rain—did they wonder if God had really spoken so long ago? After ninety years, when the boat was almost complete, did they look into the empty cages and stalls and ask themselves, "What in the world were we thinking? This is nuts!" No, we don't get any hint of their doubts. God's Word remained clear and strong. It was riveted in their minds and hearts. Sweat, opposition, and delays couldn't eradicate God's clear command.

The writer of Hebrews tells us that Noah "condemned the world." He didn't pronounce judgment on the wicked people; that was God's job. But Noah's faithful and obedient actions were a stark contrast to the wickedness of the people. He was a light in a dark world, and his light showed how utterly dark their hearts really were.

Noah didn't demand to have all the answers before he began building the ark, and he didn't require answers during construction. He just obeyed what God had instructed him to do. I can imagine people trying to interview him for a news program.

"Mr. Noah, why are you building a huge boat on dry ground?"

"Well, God told me to."

"Yes, but it doesn't make sense."

"I know."

"Does that thing float?"

"Yeah, that's the plan."

"What will it float on?"

"Uh, water."

"How much water will it take to float that thing?"

"I'd imagine quite a lot."

"Where will all that water come from?"

"Not sure."

"Rain?"

"Maybe."

"It hasn't rained here in years. Are you nuts?"

"Nope. Just doing what God told me to do."

"Don't you need to know what's going to happen before you start a project?

"No, not really. All I need is God's instruction. He'll give me more information when He thinks I need it."

May God give more of us a spirit of obedience like Noah's. We may not understand our situations, and we may not even like them, but we desperately need the faith and courage to follow through with what God tells us to do, no matter what.

Noah was a builder, not a quitter. He was faithful, not fearful. He listened to God and was "all in." He received one of the most seemingly absurd and bizarre orders ever given by God, but he didn't flinch.

His story shows us that it doesn't take a village to make a difference. Noah and his family—eight people, that's all—were faithful to God. Their tenacity, faith, and courage didn't just *shape* the destiny of every person who lived after them, it *provided* the destiny of every person who lived after them.

In the middle of the nineteenth century, many adventurous young Christian leaders sailed to the far reaches of the world to take the gospel to those who had never heard of Christ. One was Robert Jermain Thomas, who was no ordinary man. God called him to take the gospel to Korea, so he made a trip to explore the country and see if he could discern a way to make inroads into people's hearts. At that time, Korea was known as "The Hermit Kingdom." Foreigners were despised and forbidden. Thomas met opposition, but he was determined to try to reach those people. He believed God had called him to make a difference, whatever the cost.

Thomas's second trip was aboard an American naval ship. Even though land forces engaged the ship with cannon fire, Thomas wasn't deterred from his mission. With an armful of Bibles, he made his way to the beach. As a Korean soldier stabbed him with a sword, Thomas handed the man "a red book" and begged him to take it. Thomas died in the surf, giving his life for a man (and a nation) that hated him.[15]

We don't have to sail to distant countries or look back centuries to find people who are "all in," who stand in the gap for others. In our community in Chicago, gangs ruin young lives. Anthony was a gang member who attended our church, and at a men's retreat he was gloriously saved. God has given him a unique and crucial role in the lives of young men in our area. When they go through initiation rights, the gang owns them. Their whole identity is caught up in being part of that gang. If they ever want to leave the gang, they risk severe beatings, and sometimes death.

Anthony has become an advocate for gang members who want to get out of that lifestyle. Part of his ministry is to connect with gang members, love them, and share the good news of the gospel with them. If someone wants to leave that lifestyle, he meets with the gang leaders to ask for the young man's release. He tells the gang leaders, "He's trying to walk straight. Don't put a hit on him." Anthony has been there. He has earned the respect of gang leaders in Humboldt Park, and God has used him to free young men from the dead end of gang life.

You may be the only person in your family who trusts God to work in people's lives. Be strong. Don't give up. Keep believing. Keep working. Keep building. You may be the only person in your neighborhood, your school, or your workplace who is committed to exalt Jesus Christ. You will encounter opposition—some may be vicious; much will be subtle, like gossip. Be strong. Don't give up. Keep standing in that gap for the good of those around you.

MAYBE . . . JUST MAYBE

God's timing often seems agonizingly slow. We receive a promise and we trust God to honor it, but it takes forever before we begin to see the fulfillment. We're not alone in our perception of God's slowness. The prophets of Israel foretold of a Messiah who would come to save the world, but it was centuries before Jesus arrived. When Jesus was on earth, He promised to come back, but it has been two thousand years. Noah and his sons worked on the ark for 120 years before a drop of rain fell to float their boat.

When we get impatient with God, Peter gives us some perspective:

> "But do not forget this one thing, dear friends: With the Lord a day is like a thousand years, and a thousand years

> are like a day. The Lord is not slow in keeping his promise, as some understand slowness. Instead he is patient with you, not wanting anyone to perish, but everyone to come to repentance" (2 Peter 3:8–9).

Jesus said that when He returns, the condition of the world will be similar to that of Noah's time. When I put the prophecies of the Bible next to today's newspaper accounts, I wonder if we might be living in the generation of Christ's return. Many indicators are possible today for the first time since Jesus ascended after His resurrection. The nation of Israel was destroyed by the Roman legions of Titus in AD 70, and for almost 1900 years, the Jews had no homeland. But on May 8, 1948, Israel was reborn. Another prophecy says that everyone in the world will see the murder of two people in Jerusalem, and they will see Jesus in the clouds when the trumpet sounds and He returns. For hundreds of years, scholars tried to explain those statements as metaphors. But now cable news channels and the Internet make any scene on earth instantly viewable for anyone with access to a television, a smart phone, or a computer. The Middle East is ready to explode. Ancient enemies are gaining nuclear capabilities. All it would take is a small spark to ignite the region into a battle that might look a lot like the Bible's description of the last and greatest battle on earth, Armageddon.

When I mention this possibility, some people might shake their heads and say, "Ah, Pastor Choco. You're crazy! It's all just

God has called us to build our own ark, the church, amid the flood of wickedness in our culture. Who will we invite aboard? All who will come.

talk. It hasn't happened in two thousand years. Why would anyone think it could happen now?" I know, because that's exactly what I used to say. That's what they said about Noah, too. Sooner or later, it's going to happen. Jesus told us to read the signs and get ready. That's all I'm trying to do.

Evil—then and now—causes intense, undeniable pain in families, in communities, and in nations. God has called us to build our own ark, the church, amid the flood of wickedness in our culture. Who will we invite aboard? All who will come. We will offer justice for the weak and powerless, hope for the addicts, love for the abused, protection for those who are vulnerable, and God's forgiveness for the guilty.

God didn't delight in destroying the world. It broke His heart, but the cleansing flood washed away the wickedness and pain. It gave humankind a fresh start. God offers all of us a second chance, and He is incredibly patient as He awaits each person's response.

He is also asking those of us who have said yes to Him if we're "all in" like Noah. A long obedience in the same direction can't be faked—at least, not for long. When we hear God's clear call to obey, we don't trust in our own righteousness, but we bask in the mercy, grace, and love of God who clothes us in Christ's righteousness. Then, with full hearts and clear minds, we build, we serve, we give, and we care for anyone who will take our hand and join us.

Noah stood in the gap for all humankind. You and I can stand in the gap for at least a few—maybe only one.

THINK ABOUT IT . . .

1. What are the similarities and differences between Noah's culture and ours?

2. Why is it important to understand that God was deeply grieved over sin, not delighted about destroying the world?

3. Describe Noah's righteousness, blamelessness, and faithfulness. What insights from the chapter stand out to you?

4. How would you describe "a long obedience in the same direction"? Why do people quit too early? What has God called you to be and do? How have you responded?

5. What kind of fear of God is good and right and appropriate? Do you have this kind of fear? Explain your answer

6. Do you think it's wise or foolish to consider the possibility that Jesus' prediction of the conditions before His return might fit our time? If it's wise, how do you need to prepare?

7. What is God saying to you through the story of Noah?

4 DAVID

. . . was anointed by God to do the work

"So Samuel took the horn of oil and anointed [David] in the presence of his brothers, and from that day on the Spirit of the LORD came powerfully upon David" (1 Sam. 16:13).

History is sometimes viewed as phases of impersonal cultural forces (the Renaissance, the Industrial Revolution, etc.) that sometimes converge and create conflict—like Communism against democracy, or Democrats against Republicans. Certainly, ideologies and political philosophies shape events. But when we look closely, we inevitably find a person or a small group of people who had the courage to do whatever was needed—often at great personal risk and sacrifice—for a cause they believed in. Sometimes, those people had positions of prominence before stepping up to champion a cause, but often they rose from obscurity to courageously stand in the gap.

We look back at David as the greatest king of Israel . . . the greatest until the promised King, the Son of David, appeared a millennium later. At first, though, even his own family didn't believe in him. He was a nobody—overlooked, despised, and forsaken. He wasn't even a champion under his own roof!

THEN AND NOW

David was born into a world where God's people were distressed and discouraged. The Philistines and other enemies had been attacking their settlements. The brutal Philistines had been around for centuries, but had been especially ruthless during the period of the judges. The people of Israel were tired of being assaulted over and over again, so they asked God for a king. They wanted to be like all the other nations. They wanted a man to rule over them, not God.

When they would not be dissuaded, God gave them exactly what they asked for. He anointed the tall and handsome Saul to be their first king. For a while, Saul's rule looked promising, but he soon proved that he wasn't up to the task. When the mighty Philistine army arrayed against Saul and his terrified men, Saul could have waited patiently as God had instructed (1 Sam. 10:8). Instead, he panicked and took the matter into his own hands (1 Sam. 13:5–14).

A gap is a place of weakness, vulnerability, and danger. At that moment in their history, the people of God were in a huge gap! Their survival hung in the balance. They were demoralized, broken, and hopeless. As the Philistine army took positions across the valley, the destiny of God's people was in jeopardy. Saul had proven that he wasn't a capable leader, but he was still in command. The situation looked hopeless.

God values justice, mercy, and love. When we neglect those things, our culture suffers devastating gaps.

Broken hearts and broken societies can occur when God's standards aren't valued. Racism, immigration restrictions, economic policy, prayer in schools, neglect of the homeless, and many other society-wide issues don't get the attention they deserve. God values justice, mercy, and love. When we neglect those things, our culture suffers devastating gaps. We're broken, downcast, and vulnerable. Gradual decay produces heartache as much as a violent outburst, but it's easier to shrug off because it has been going on for so long . . . and no one seems to care.

We aren't facing off against the Philistine army today, but we face other enemies:

- The poverty rate is alarmingly high in the richest culture in the world.
- One in five children in America goes to bed hungry every night.
- Malnutrition affects almost one-third of the children in developing countries.[16]

- Over three million kids drop out of high school each year,[17] and many who graduate can barely read.
- We used to bemoan that one in two marriages end in divorce, but now many couples don't even bother to get married. They change partners like they trade cars.
- Twenty years ago our culture was deeply divided over abortion, but today millions of babies die with barely a word of protest.
- A decade ago, domestic violence and pornography were important topics, but today, those concerns are overshadowed by the millions of girls who are victims of human trafficking.
- Only a few years ago, leaders debated the issue of teaching sexual abstinence in schools, but today sexual activity among kids is almost taken for granted.
- A few decades ago our nation's focus was on civil rights; today it is on protecting gay rights.
- We once debated having prayer in schools, but now we're raising a generation of kids who get their "truth" from violent, hip-hop lyrics.
- In the 1950s, 76 percent of high school students said they feared God. By 2000, only 4 percent said they feared God. In other words, 96 percent of the kids coming out of our high schools today don't respect God, and by extension, they don't respect any other authority.

- In a recent year, America deported 409,849 immigrants, tearing apart the fabric of families and communities.[18]

At the height of the Cold War in 1955, President Eisenhower prepared to go to the Geneva Peace Conference to meet with the Soviet leaders. Both countries had developed hydrogen bombs that were far more powerful than the atomic bombs that fell on Japan at the end of World War II. Many people believed humanity was only one mistake away from complete, worldwide destruction. Before leaving for the conference, the president appeared on national television to urge people to go to church and pray for peace. That kind of plea from a national leader was common then; it is unimaginable now.

We face a tsunami of immorality crashing throughout our land. Only a generation ago, Christians defined the culture, but now we are perceived as out of step with the culture. The mainstream media depicts us as against gay marriage. Do they realize we're also against discrimination, human trafficking, gang violence, racism, hatred, and abuse? Do they know what we're *for*, as well as what we're *against*? Do they know we're for love, forgiveness, reconciliation, justice, and mercy? In response to criticism, many believers have withdrawn and become the silent minority. We have become marginalized citizens. People no longer care what we think or believe.

Those who stand up for God's justice and truth inevitably become targets . . . for somebody, right or left on the political or religious spectrums. Remaining quiet may limit our exposure to criticism, but it can be the coward's way out. There are times when we can't let opposition stop us. We simply have to stand up and represent God in our communities.

I went to our state capitol to speak in opposition to a bill authorizing same-sex marriage. Some in the legislature accused me of hating homosexuals. That's not true at all. I love people of all colors, all ethnic backgrounds, all ages, all socioeconomic groups, and all sexual preferences. I love rich businesspeople and death-row prisoners, movie stars and those who live on the streets, the most conscientious pastors and the addicts and prostitutes, police officers and gang bangers. Every person is precious in God's sight, although that doesn't make everyone's behavior good, right, and profitable for the community.

We live in a pluralistic nation. I get that. But we have to be able to draw a line between right and wrong. Without that line culture descends into chaos, and gay marriage crosses that line. The Bible allows a lot of latitude in many, many areas. People can debate numerous issues and find different legitimate perspectives in the Scriptures. But a few issues are crystal clear. All three of the ancient religions that find their source in Abraham's call agree that God decreed marriage to be between one man and one woman. My position has its roots in thousands of years of faith and history.

When the Illinois lawmakers found out I was coming to speak about the bill, some of them tried to prevent me from speaking and another tried to offer me a deal to shut me up. One of the representatives who knows me laughed at the proposed offer and told the man, "You don't know Choco. He can't be bought. Get ready. He's coming, and he's speaking the truth!"

When I speak on gay marriage—or abortion or immigration or guns or any other hot topic in our society—I'm well aware that I will be stigmatized and caricatured by those who oppose my views. They try to paint me as narrow-minded, angry, and uncaring. One of my ongoing goals, then, is to make sure I communicate a heart of compassion, reason, and kindness as I talk about God's clear directives from the Bible.

Social activism isn't just a hobby for believers. We get involved in the big issues of our times because we represent the King and His purposes on earth. Because of negative representations in movies and in the news, many Americans see Christians as judgmental, hypocritical, and moralistic—trying to impose our values instead of living as beautiful lights on a hill. We need nonbelievers to see how much we care for the lost, the homeless, the downcast, the hungry, the sick, and the prisoners.

Noted scholar N. T. Wright has said that if Christians stopped caring for hurting people, society would come apart at the seams. The central message of the Christian faith—Christ's death and resurrection—gives us hope in the future and motivation for action today. In his book, *Surprised by Hope,* Wright comments:

> "The point of the resurrection . . . is that *the present bodily life is not valueless just because it will die.* . . . What you do with your body in the present matters because God has a great future in store for it. . . .What you *do* in the present—by painting, preaching, singing, sewing, praying, teaching, building hospitals, digging wells, campaigning for justice, writing poems, caring for the needy, loving your neighbor as yourself—*will last into God's future.* These activities are not simply ways of making the present life a little less beastly, a little more bearable, until the day when we leave it behind altogether. . . . They are part of what we may call *building for God's kingdom.*"[19]

The circumstances for the Israelites three thousand years ago were extremely different from today, but the results were similar. Too many people were overlooked. Leaders began with tremendous promise but failed to deliver on their lofty goals. In the towns and in the streets of the city, people felt neglected. They feared injustice because they had seen too many instances when their leaders hadn't upheld God's values. The people were discouraged. Many had simply given up. Into this yawning gap, God told the prophet Samuel to go to Jesse's house. There, he would anoint a new king of Israel.

AN UNLIKELY CANDIDATE

Samuel's assignment was not as simple as it might sound. The prophet was afraid for his life (1 Sam. 16:1–2). What if King Saul found out he was going to anoint a new king? And besides, Samuel didn't even know which of Jesse's sons God had chosen. The faithful prophet hadn't counted on fear and confusion as part of his job description! When he arrived at the house, he asked Jesse to bring his sons to see him. One by one, from oldest to youngest, Samuel examined them. Each time God said, "No, not this one." Seven sons arrived, were inspected, and were rejected. Samuel asked Jesse, "Are these all the sons you have?" (1 Sam. 16:11)

Jesse explained that there was only one more—the youngest, who was out in the fields on shepherd duty. The look on his face probably said, "Surely you don't want to see him! He smells like sheep, and besides, he's not as gifted as my other sons."

Think about Jesse's statement. The most respected, powerful spiritual leader in the nation had come to his house and asked to meet his sons. Jesse apparently thought so little about David that he wasn't even invited to the meeting! David wasn't just an obscure figure in the nation; he was obscure in his own family.

When we see talented young men and women, we often say, "He has a lot of promise!" or "She's going to go a long way in life!" David's dad had no such vision for his youngest son. He seems to have considered David a distraction, a liability. He was so ashamed of him that he didn't even number him among his sons.

David's parents didn't see greatness in him, and his brothers didn't see the spark of glory in their sibling. Perhaps David didn't see it in himself, either. But God did. He told Samuel, "The LORD does not look at the things people look at. People look at the outward appearance, but the LORD looks at the heart" (1 Sam. 16:7). The prophet anointed the boy as the new king of Israel, but he wouldn't take the throne that day (or anytime soon). The anointing prepared him for his all-important role, but not yet . . . not yet.

Throughout the Bible, we see that God chooses to use the weak, the outcasts, and the powerless to accomplish His purposes.

Throughout the Bible, we see that God chooses to use the weak, the outcasts, and the powerless to accomplish His purposes. Abraham was fearful and lied to save his own skin; Gideon was a coward; Mary was a poor peasant girl; and Jesus' disciples had no formal training. God sometimes uses strong people, but first He humbles them. Moses thought he would take a stand for the Hebrew people, so he murdered an Egyptian overseer. For the next forty years he lived a humble life of a shepherd on the backside of nowhere until God called him to deliver his people from slavery. Jacob was a cunning dealmaker, but God took him to the end of himself to teach him authentic faith and trust. Paul was an up-and-coming star of the anti-Christian movement when

Jesus appeared to him on the road to Damascus. The encounter shattered and humbled a proud, angry man, and God shaped him into a humble, dependent follower.

Whether they begin as humble or arrogant, God uses pliable people to accomplish His purposes. He calls men and women who are willing to say, "Not my will, but Yours. Not my comfort, but sacrifice. Not my glory, but Your honor."

Believers throughout history have faced those hard choices. One of the most remarkable was a second-century leader named Polycarp. He grew up like David: an overlooked nobody who wasn't on anyone's list of "most likely to succeed." He had little if any formal education. His childhood offered no promise of greatness, but Polycarp grew to be a man of humility, spiritual strength, and courage.

During his life, the Christian faith was assailed by the doctrine of Gnosticism, the erroneous belief that only a select group of super-spiritual people could connect with God. Anyone outside their tight circle had no chance of salvation. Polycarp successfully defended the deity of Christ and the glory of the gospel. Many former Gnostics came to faith in Jesus because of him. But believers faced another problem in addition to heresies: the wrath of the Roman Empire. Christians who lived in the Empire were given a choice: proclaim Caesar as Lord, and live, or proclaim Jesus as Lord, and die. Caesar crucified thousands of them, had many torn apart by wild animals for entertainment, and had others covered with tar and set on fire to light his parties. When Polycarp was eighty-six years old, Roman guards escorted him to the floor of the Coliseum. He was told to deny Christ or die. He heard a voice from heaven telling him, "Be strong and play the man, Polycarp."

The Roman governor, Statius Quadratus, insisted, "Take the oath to Caesar, and you will be set free. Curse Christ."

The old man replied, "For eighty-six years I have been His servant, and He has never done me wrong. How can I blaspheme my King who saved me?"

The governor became enraged. He threatened to throw the old man to the wild beasts or burn him at the stake. Even with violent death imminent, Polycarp refused to turn his back on Jesus. He calmly replied, "But why do you delay? Come, do what you will."

The governor directed the soldiers to nail the old man to a stake and light the fires. Polycarp stepped up to the stake but waved off the guards. Remarkably, he gave them instructions: "Leave me as I am. For He who grants me to endure the fire will enable me also to remain on the pyre unmoved, without the security you desire from nails." Soon, the fire consumed him.

Polycarp's amazing courage in the face of torture and death inspired the Christians and amazed the pagans. An account of the impact of his death reports, "He is even spoken of by the heathen in every place."[20]

David stands in a long line of people who at some point in their lives were unknown to men but well known to God. He later became Israel's most beloved king, but he began as an outcast, overlooked and despised by his father and his brothers.

David stands in a long line of people who at some point in their lives were unknown to men but well known to God.

BEHIND THE SCENES

From Jesse's actions when Samuel visited his home, we can conclude that he hadn't spent much time training David for a fulfilling life. The other sons got preferential treatment from their dad, but God had a special curriculum for David. Shepherding provided an education that other jobs did not. In Palestine in David's time, lions and bears roamed the countryside. When the flock was attacked and one of those beasts carried off a sheep, a good shepherd didn't just shrug his shoulders or hide in the bushes. David had faced those challenges: "I went after [the lion or bear], struck it and rescued the sheep from its mouth. When it turned on me, I seized it by its hair, struck it and killed it" (1 Sam. 17:35).

David had killed at least one lion and bear with his bare hands! After a couple of such encounters, he may have wondered, *What's going on? Nobody else in Israel has this many attacks by wild animals!* But David's shepherding lessons were all part of

God's plan to prepare him to stand in the gap in one of the most famous encounters of all time between good and evil. God was preparing David in private. Later He would use him in front of a large crowd.

NO ORDINARY DAY

Israel was beset by various enemies during this time. One group, the Amalekites, had tormented God's people for centuries. God gave Saul clear instructions to wipe out the Amalekites, sparing no one, not even animals (1 Sam. 15:1–3). Saul attacked and defeated the Amalekites, but in direct defiance to God he spared their king and the best of their flocks. That was a turning point when God rejected Saul as king, when Samuel anointed David, and when Saul's army began to lose confidence in him.

No sooner had the Amalekite threat been dissolved than an even fiercer army showed up to fight Israel: the Philistines. With Saul's reputation shaken and his army weak, the timing couldn't have been worse.

To avoid full-scale warfare, ancient rival kings sometimes sent out champion soldiers for man-to-man combat, winner take all. It was "trial by battle ordeal." The Philistines had that in mind when they sent out their champion, a giant named Goliath.

The sight of the giant caused Israel's soldiers' blood to run cold. The Bible describes him this way:

> "His height was six cubits and a span. He had a bronze helmet on his head and wore a coat of scale armor of bronze weighing five thousand shekels; on his legs he wore bronze greaves, and a bronze javelin was slung on his back. His spear shaft was like a weaver's rod, and its iron point weighed six hundred shekels. His shield bearer went ahead of him" (1 Sam. 17:4–7).

Day after day, Goliath strode out to the plain between the two armies and taunted Saul and his soldiers with the same challenge: choose one person for combat. If the Israelite soldier won, the Philistines would become slaves of Israel. But if Goliath won, the Israelites would be subject to the Philistines. I can imagine Saul's soldiers looking at each other when Goliath snorted, "This day I defy the armies of Israel! Give me a man and let us fight each other!" (1 Sam. 17:10) Their expressions surely said, "Hey, you can go out there and fight him, but I'm not going!"

For forty days, morning and evening, the giant taunted God's army. No one volunteered to fight him. Saul may have tried to enlist a brave man to represent him and his people, but he found no takers. Among the quaking Israelite soldiers were Jesse's three oldest sons—Eliab, Abinadab, and Shammah—who had joined the army to fight under King Saul.

David now had two thankless jobs. He continued to have shepherding responsibilities, and he also became an errand boy to carry supplies to his brothers. As it so happened, Jesse had given him bread and cheese (basically, the ingredients for cheese sandwiches) to carry to the front line, and David arrived just as the armies formed lines of battle as they did every day before Goliath issued his challenge.

This was the first time David had seen and heard the defiant, mocking Philistine giant. But David saw more than that. He also witnessed Israel's soldiers not just retreating, but running for their lives! They didn't want to get near the monster!

When David heard Goliath's threats, the giant's words must have sounded very familiar. He had heard similar mocking from his own brothers. Goliath's sneers sounded like home. For years, David had endured his brother's taunts day after day. In response, he didn't back down in fear, and he didn't collapse in self-pity. He got stronger. God used his dysfunctional background to prepare David's life. His brothers meant their cruel words for evil, but God used them for good.

David took stock of his opponent as he had with the previous threats of the bear and the lion. He wanted to know, "Who is this uncircumcised Philistine that he should defy the armies of the living God?" (1 Sam. 17:26) If David had been from my neighborhood, he would have asked, "Who is that punk?"

Saul and his entire army were terrified; David was courageous. Saul saw an awesome enemy; David saw an opportunity.

Saul needed an *ish* (man) to stand in the *habinayim* (between two camps for combat). David was determined to be that *ish*!

David asked a couple of questions to clarify the situation and the promised reward. At that moment, his brother Eliab walked up and overheard him. We can imagine their previous dinner conversations for many years when we read Eliab's reaction to David's honest questions. He was furious! He snarled, "Why have you come down here? And with whom did you leave those few sheep in the wilderness? I know how conceited you are and how wicked your heart is; you came down only to watch the battle" (1 Sam. 17:28).

Undoubtedly, David was hurt by his brother's verbal assault, but he didn't back down. He turned to someone else for some answers. Men standing nearby were surprised to hear anyone talk about the possibility of fighting—and killing—the giant. They immediately went to Saul to tell him about the new kid in the camp.

Saul sent for David. When he arrived at Saul's tent, we don't hear the king initiate the conversation. David immediately assured Saul, "Let no one lose heart on account of this Philistine; your servant will go and fight him" (1 Sam. 17:32).

Saul scoffed (I paraphrase here), "Um, have you looked in the mirror? You're only a kid. You can't beat that giant!"

David realized this struggle wasn't just against flesh and blood. Something much bigger was at stake: the reputation of God. The giant wasn't merely threatening some soldiers; his defiance was against Israel's God. David explained to Saul:

> "Your servant has killed both the lion and the bear; this uncircumcised Philistine will be like one of them, because he has defied the armies of the living God. The LORD who rescued me from the paw of the lion and the paw of the bear will rescue me from the hand of this Philistine" (1 Sam. 17:36–37).

After forty days of Goliath's taunts, Saul must have been absolutely desperate because he agreed to let this kid represent him and his army in mortal combat. He gave David the green light to go out and fight the Philistine giant, but first he offered the boy his tunic and his armor. David tried them on, which must have been a comical sight. Saul was very tall; David, not so tall. Saul was a trained soldier with tailored armor; David had never worn armor in his life.

David politely passed on Saul's offer, picked up his shepherd's staff, and headed toward the battlefield. Along the way he selected five smooth stones from a streambed and put them in his pouch. With his staff in one hand and a sling in the other, he walked out onto the plain between the two armies. Imagine this: David left his home that morning already prepared for the fight of his life without even knowing it. He carried his staff and sling because he understood he might encounter threats at any moment. He came prepared to lead and to fight.

At that moment, which side would you have wanted to be on? Would you have staked your life on the kid with the sling and the stick? Or would you rather have stood behind the giant with the powerful weapons, massive muscles, and strong armor? I'm not a betting man, but I can imagine the betting line at Las Vegas would have been huge!

Think about the Philistine army as the giant and the kid approached each other. They must have been licking their chops, anticipating the slaughter and plunder they would enjoy in a few minutes. And think of the men in Saul's army. They hadn't been able to find a trained, skilled warrior in forty days to fight Goliath, so now they were sending out a boy with a stick, a sling, and a few little rocks. They were either writing their wills or looking for an escape route!

At that moment, the gap of weakness, vulnerability, and danger looked very, very wide.

David had no such anxiety. He knew exactly what he was going to do. Goliath looked at the boy and sneered, "Am I a dog, that you come at me with sticks? . . . Come here, and I'll give your flesh to the birds and the wild animals!" (1 Sam. 17:43–44)

David wasn't terrified, nor was he tongue-tied. As he advanced, he told the giant and everyone who was listening:

> "You come against me with sword and spear and javelin, but I come against you in the name of the LORD Almighty, the God of the armies of Israel, whom you have defied. This day the LORD will deliver you into my hands, and I'll strike you down and cut off your head. This very day I will give the carcasses of the Philistine army to the birds and the wild animals, and the whole world will know that there is a God in Israel. All those gathered here will know that it is not by sword or spear that the LORD saves; for the battle is the LORD's, and he will give all of you into our hands" (1 Sam. 17:45–47).

Every child in Sunday school knows what happened next. David took a stone out of his pouch, put it in his sling, and slung it with all his skill and might. It hit Goliath squarely in the forehead. He fell to the ground with the force of an earthquake. David took the giant's sword and cut off his head. But most people miss the rest of the story. The Bible says that after David cut off the head of the giant, the army of Israel surged forward.

I've seen dramatic and unexpected endings to football and basketball games, and I've seen game-winning, ninth-inning homeruns. But nothing in the annals of sports or warfare was as unexpected as the boy walking onto the field of battle and killing the defiant giant.

Saul's army pursued the Philistines and then returned to plunder their campsites. How stunning was that to everyone?

When it was all over, Saul asked his commanding general, "Whose kid was that?"

The general replied, "I don't know."

MAYBE YOU . . . MAYBE ME

Earlier that morning, David had been a nobody. His father hadn't even considered him to be one of his sons when the prophet Samuel came for a visit. David was just an errand boy for his dad, and his brothers despised him. The only ones who respected him were the sheep he protected and the wild animals that knew better than to mess with him! But God had seen something in David's heart. He saw greatness where others saw nothing.

God had seen something in David's heart. He saw greatness where others saw nothing.

David's anointing occurred prior to this event, not after. God's anointing doesn't wait until we *prove* ourselves by doing something dramatic for Him. God sees into our hearts, and His anointing *prepares* us to do great things for Him.

After his anointing, David didn't demand attention, and he didn't walk into Saul's throne room and say, "Get out. It's my turn now." David kept tending sheep, serving his father, and running errands to help his brothers. For a while, it didn't appear that

God's anointing would make any difference at all. But it made all the difference in the world! David was ready for one of the biggest tests anyone has ever faced.

That day in the gap between the two armies, David responded to a desperate situation with faith and strength. When he heard the giant's taunts and discovered no one had faced him for forty long days, he could have said, "Hey, I just brought some cheese sandwiches. This isn't my fight!" Instead, David's heart was galvanized by the threat. He ran into danger instead of away from it. He grabbed the situation by the throat instead of hiding in fear.

David realized that threats in our society don't just mock flesh and blood. They are part of a spiritual battle for the souls of men and women . . . and the heart of our culture. Giants in our families and in our communities mock God. They claim, "God doesn't care. God's standards don't matter. What difference does God make anyway?"

David saw beyond the existential threat of a big, ugly soldier and realized the reputation of God was on the line. For forty days, Saul and his army had let unbelievers mock His love, power, and purpose. David's heart and his actions yelled, "No more! God is able. Just watch and see Him at work!"

Goliath wasn't enormous when he was born. Similarly, many of the problems in our families, communities, and culture start small and grow over time. They build up and threaten to overwhelm us because no one did anything about them when they had earlier opportunities. God had instructed His people to wipe out the Amalekites generations earlier when they entered the Promised Land, but they didn't finish the job. Saul's battle against those enemies depleted Israel's limited forces. And Saul didn't obey God and finish the job when *he* had the chance. His failure was extremely costly for his army's morale and their trust in him.

With those failures in their background, Saul and his army felt weak, afraid, and demoralized. No one had the courage to face the giant who mocked them twice a day—no one but the outcast, despised shepherd, David.

Sarah is a woman in our community who knows something about desperate situations. Her husband was arrested for selling drugs and assaulting a police officer. She found herself faced with the challenge of raising three children on her own—with the stigma of having a husband in prison. For several years, she and her kids lived hand to mouth . . . and then her situation got worse. She was in a gang and wasn't a caring mom to her kids. Sarah and her children were on the streets much of the time—destitute and angry.

Some people from our church invited Sarah to come to our services and feel our love for her. There she met Christ and was changed from the inside out. Instead of giving up in self-pity and despair, Sarah began to see her condition as an opportunity to reach out to other women whose husbands are incarcerated. When she found out a woman's husband was in prison, she contacted her and offered to take her to visit her husband. Over the years, Sarah's kindness and consistency have enabled her to give new hope to women who thought their lives were over. Through her efforts, dozens of families have remained intact during the most difficult seasons of their lives. Prison—along with loneliness, poverty, and hopelessness—were giants to these families, but Sarah stepped in with the sling and stone of God's tender love.

David's *courage* was the result of his *confidence* in a powerful, wise, loving God.

When we read the story of David killing Goliath, we often focus on the young man's courage. We need to dig a little deeper. David's *courage* was the result of his *confidence* in a powerful, wise, loving God. If we try to emulate his courage without diving deeply into the wonder of God's might and grace, eventually we will be crushed because we can't continually manufacture that kind of courage on our own. If, however, we focus our attention in the same place David focused, our confidence in God will produce genuine courage to face any giant in our lives.

Ironically—and beautifully—the loop of faith was closed a thousand years later when David's God, the promised Messiah, the Son of David, appeared as both King and Savior.

David trusted in the God of the promise; we trust in the God revealed in Jesus, the Messiah, the great Davidic King.

What are the giants in your world? Think carefully. Don't make too many assumptions. David saw and heard what everyone else saw and heard, but he had faith to believe that *this* giant was *his* giant to slay.

People are watching to see if you will hurl the stones and cut the head off the giant in your world. Like Saul's army, they will surge forward if they know they have a champion of their cause. In our nation, battles are taking place in the courts, in congress, in state legislatures, and in voting booths. Many laws have been passed in recent years that are against God's commands and values. But just because something is declared "legal" doesn't mean it is ethical.

When we hear a giant's taunts, we need to gather information and then take action. Only rarely can we slay a giant in a single day. Far more often we need tenacity and wisdom as much as we need boldness. We need faith in God, no matter what the outcome may be.

A gap is a place of weakness. I never felt weaker than when our church found itself with nowhere to go, no place to call home. We had been renting a school auditorium for over eight years when school administrators asked us to vacate for the summer for remodeling. They offered us another school auditorium, but it wasn't in our community. I felt frustrated and defeated. I heard mockers saying, "You should have moved the church out of the city. There's no land in the city, and any land you find will be too expensive!"

I pleaded with God, "I need to hear from You soon!" I felt as though I was leading people out into the wilderness. When I made the connection between our situation and the children of Israel wandering in the desert, I suggested, "Okay, if we're going to be in the wilderness, let's build a tent." And that's exactly what we did. We built a tent and held services in it for three months. It was both wonderful and challenging at the same time. We experienced the powerful presence of God as I taught a series on the tabernacle as it is described in Exodus.

During these months, we were humbled, exhausted, and totally surrendered to God. That summer we endured a thunderstorm, lots of rain and mud, a heat wave, and even a violent hailstorm. Some people didn't like the challenge of using a tent as a place of worship. With a broken heart, I watched some of our families leave and go to other churches. But it was at this very time that God answered our prayers to provide a place for us. A few days after I made my desperate prayer to God, one of our members called me to say, "An old warehouse on Division Street just went on the market."

I responded, "Let's go see it!"

A month later we purchased the land. The following year we tore down the existing warehouse and began to build. Today as I write, it has been a month since our grand opening celebration.

Standing against negativity, frustration, and doubt was difficult, but it can't compare to the awesome feeling of knowing you can trust God with the biggest challenges in your life.

If we demand the answer we expect and must have it now, we will whine and complain when problems aren't resolved quickly and completely. Important issues almost always require a long and complex process, and we can expect others to show a blend of opposition and ignorance as we tackle the problems.

Think about the Gospel accounts of the life of Jesus. He was the ultimate David, the chosen King, the promised Messiah of David's lineage. But throughout His ministry, the religious elite opposed Him and His disciples consistently misunderstood Him. When He was finally arrested, His closest followers ran for their lives! Only after His resurrection and the coming of the Spirit at Pentecost do we see the kind of courage and wisdom needed to change the culture. Through justice, mercy, love, and sacrifice, the number of Christians grew from about 6 percent to 50 percent by the fourth century.[21]

Today our families and our culture are looking for someone anointed by the Spirit to step into the enormous gaps. They're looking for someone like David who is willing to take on the Goliaths around us. They're looking for you and me.

Martin Luther King, Jr. is one of my heroes. Few people in history have shown such faith, courage, love, wisdom, and tenacity. He remarked,

> "Courage is an inner resolution to go forward despite obstacles; cowardice is submissive surrender to circumstances. Courage breeds creativity; cowardice represses fear and is mastered by it. Cowardice asks the question, is it safe? Expediency asks the question, is it politic? Vanity asks the question, is it popular? But conscience asks the question, is it right? And there comes a time when we must take a position that is neither safe, nor politic, nor popular, but one must take it because it is right."[22]

There are giants in our lives, our families, and our communities today. Like the soldiers in Saul's army, we've heard their taunts so long that we've gotten used to them. And we've gotten used to hiding in fear. But it's time to do something about them. If we don't kill them, they will kill us. It's time to be God's *ish* or *isha*.

When we stand up to our giants, we're risking everything. It's not safe, and it's often not politically correct. Many people will oppose us because we're rocking the boat. If *we* don't stand for righteousness and justice in our generation, someone else will have to come along and find the courage, but by then the situation will be even worse. Let's not put courage off on the next generation. Let's stand in the gap now, today, in this moment when the giants roar. They look menacing, but they're punks. God is far wiser, stronger, and more righteous than any enemy. Let's trust Him and break open the gates of hell for His glory and for His people.

THINK ABOUT IT . . .

1. What are some Goliaths in your family? . . . in your community? . . . in our country?

2. Why is it important to see David as an outcast before we see him on the scene killing Goliath and later becoming king?

3. How did God use David's experiences with lions and bears before he fought Goliath? What were the similarities between the wild animals and the giant? What are some differences?

4. What are some challenging experiences you've had that have prepared you (or are preparing you) to fight the giants around you?

5. David saw the giant as more than a physical menace. What difference does it make to realize the giants in our families and our nation are part of a spiritual battle against the forces of darkness?

6. What are some reasons it's so easy to avoid facing the giants and assume someone else (if anyone) will fight them?

7. Explain the importance of God's anointing as preparation for future action.

8. What is God saying to you through the story of David?

5 BARNABAS

. . . saw hidden potential

"Then Barnabas went to Tarsus to look for Saul, and when he found him, he brought him to Antioch. So for a whole year Barnabas and Saul met with the church and taught great numbers of people. The disciples were called Christians first at Antioch" (Acts 11:25–26).

A lot of people believe Murphy's Law is the central, driving principle of the universe. The law says, "If anything can go wrong, it will." Of course, those who hold Murphy to be the source of insight about life can point to a million examples to prove their point:

- The other line at the grocery store always moves faster.
- There's always one ingredient for the recipe that's missing from your pantry.
- Any tool dropped while you're working on your car rolls underneath to the exact center where it's hardest to reach.
- Company uniforms come in two sizes: too small and too large.

- If you lose a needle, someone's foot will find it.
- To get a loan at the bank, you have to prove that you don't need it.
- In schools, disasters inevitably occur when visitors are in the room.
- Every food you crave is bad for you.
- You realize it's the third Thursday of the month after you climb three flights of stairs! (I have to stop here to explain this inside joke. Our staff members have to walk up three long flights of steps to our offices. When they forget it's the assigned day of the month for our street cleaning, they have to go move their cars and walk up again because Chicago sets the world record for writing parking tickets.)

Do you know people who live by Murphy's Law? They can find something wrong with a bowl of ice cream or a puppy, and they drag others down with them. Do you see a person like that when you look in the mirror?

Christians have the honor to stand in the gap to be a source of light, life, and hope for those around them. No matter what difficulty or calamity we face, those who have experienced the transforming grace of Jesus Christ should overflow with joy, love, and optimism. We don't subscribe to blind optimism that denies the reality of suffering and setbacks, but rather hold out for a strong hope in a great and loving God who will make all things—yes, *all* things—work together for good for those who love Him.

Some of us are naturally "glass half-full" people. We look for the good in people and in situations. But many of us are "glass half-empty" people who see only the negative and overlook the possibilities. God knows we need to be reminded to look for the good. We need encouragement.

To *encourage* means to put courage into someone who is weak and vulnerable. In Greek, the word is *paraklesis*, "to come alongside." This is the word Jesus used when He promised "another Counselor." The Holy Spirit comes alongside to counsel, comfort, inspire, and guide us. As we receive encouragement, we can pour it out into the lives of those who are struggling.

The Bible is full of instructions to refocus our hearts so we have a more positive impact on those around us. For example, Paul wrote, "Therefore encourage one another and build each other up" (1 Thess. 5:11). When people are isolated, they can drift into depression. The writer to the Hebrews reminds us, "Let us consider how we may spur one another on toward love and good deeds, not giving up meeting together, as some are in the habit of doing, but encouraging one another" (Heb. 10:24–25).

All of us need to hang around others who encourage us, those who inject hope when we feel hopeless, faith when we're faithless, and love when we feel unlovable. Even the strongest "gap people" need encouragement to be the people God wants them to be. Nehemiah needed the king to believe in him. Esther needed Mordecai to help her seize her moment of destiny. Noah needed his sons to work alongside him in building the ark. David needed Samuel's affirmation to realize his potential.

One of the greatest leaders the church has ever known was the apostle Paul. Early in his career, he found himself in a gap—a place of vulnerability, weakness, and danger. He desperately needed someone to stand in the gap for him.

AND YOU THINK YOU'VE GOT IT ROUGH!

The first days and weeks after the Holy Spirit came at Pentecost were electric. That day only 120 people were in the upper room, waiting as Jesus had instructed, but when the Spirit fell on them, they changed the world! Thousands of people responded to the message of the gospel of grace (Acts 1–2). And those new believers didn't just sit in pews (partly because they didn't have pews back then). They spread the news of Jesus to every region around them, and they shared their possessions to care for those in need. Grace and generosity—those were the traits of the early believers (Acts 4:32–37).

When the Pharisees and Romans killed Jesus, they assumed His followers would melt into the scenery because that's what had happened every other time someone tried to lead a revolution. This time, however, it was different: the movement grew!

We can imagine the Jewish and Roman leaders' relief on the Saturday after Jesus was executed. Finally, they were sure, all the fuss was over. But a few days later they heard ominous reports that Jesus had appeared to people—not just one or two, but to 500 at one time! In the weeks that followed, Jesus' closest followers stood up to preach that He had come back to life, and that He was Jehovah God . . . their God!

The ruling elite had felt threatened by Jesus and the few who followed Him. Now they were even more threatened because far more people were getting involved! They dragged Peter and John before the Sanhedrin, the Jewish senate, and they were astonished by the unschooled fisherman's eloquent defense of faith in Jesus. Later, the party of the Sadducees was jealous of the apostles' popularity, so they had all of them arrested and imprisoned. The Lord sent an angel to free them. The next day the Sadducees looked for them in the cell, but the apostles were preaching in the temple courts! They were arrested again, and Peter gave another brilliant defense. The Sadducees wanted to execute them all, but one of their leaders persuaded them to let the apostles go . . . for now.

Before long a deacon named Stephen was arrested for preaching about Jesus. At his trial, he gave the Jewish elders a long explanation of the history of faith—the history of *their* faith—and how it pointed directly to Jesus Christ. When he finished, they sentenced him to death by stoning. As the men picked up rocks, they took off their cloaks and put them at the feet of one of the fiercest leaders, Saul of Tarsus.

Stephen's execution led to widespread persecution of Christians. Many believers fled from Jerusalem to towns and cities throughout Judea and Samaria. In Luke's account of the early church, he tells us, "Godly men buried Stephen and mourned deeply for him. But Saul began to destroy the church. Going from house to house, he dragged off men and women and put them in prison" (Acts 8:2–3).

In his almost obsessive search for Christians, Saul set out for Damascus. He planned to arrest a lot of them there. On the way, however, his trip was interrupted when Jesus appeared to him in a blinding light. Blinded by the light of God's glory and grace, Saul stumbled into Damascus—as a humbled new believer in Jesus Christ instead of Jesus' archenemy.

After Saul's sight was restored and he was baptized, he went to the local synagogue to preach. His message was the opposite of what everyone expected. Instead of denying Jesus and threatening those who followed Him, he preached that Jesus is the Son of God!

> "All those who heard him were astonished and asked, 'Isn't he the man who raised havoc in Jerusalem among those who call on this name? And hasn't he come here to take them as prisoners to the chief priests?' Yet Saul grew more and more powerful and baffled the Jews

> living in Damascus by proving that Jesus is the Messiah" (Acts 9:21–22).

Saul was in a sticky predicament. The Jews, his former allies, now conspired to kill him. In a dramatic escape, a few men lowered Saul in a basket through a hole in the city wall. He was safe from the Jews, but he had another problem: the Christians didn't believe his conversion was genuine. At this critical moment in his life—and in the history of the Christian movement—the Jews hated Saul and accused him of betraying them, and the Christians were too terrified to trust him.

ALL IN A NAME

When Saul returned to Jerusalem, he was a man without a country, without friends, and without a home. He tried to meet with the leaders of the church, but they must have been saying to each other, "Does he think we have amnesia? He was trying to capture and kill us just the other day!"

At that moment, a man named Barnabas stepped up. He heard Saul's story about what had happened on the road to Damascus, his preaching in the city, and his escape, and he believed every word. He went with Saul to the apostles and spoke up for his new friend. Barnabas had street credibility. The apostles knew he was a man of integrity and wisdom, so they took his word for Saul.

As soon as Saul began to speak out in Jerusalem about Jesus, some Greek Jews became incensed and tried to kill him. At that point the apostles took steps to defend their new brother in Christ. They escorted him to the coast, and he took a ship north to Tarsus, his hometown.

Later Saul became the writer of much of the New Testament, the man who planted churches across the Roman Empire, and probably the greatest leader the church has ever known. But if it hadn't been for Barnabas, who knows how different Saul's life might have been?

If it hadn't been for Barnabas, who knows how different Saul's life might have been?

Luke introduces us to Barnabas in the first chapters of Acts. His Jewish name was Joseph. He was a priest, a Levite from Cyprus. His impact on others was so positive that he earned a nickname that stuck: Barnabas. In Greek, *bar* means "son of," and *nabas* means "encouragement." This guy was known as "Son of Encouragement."

In the early days of the church, many people had come from distant lands for the Jewish feast of Pentecost. When they heard the message of the gospel and sensed the excitement of knowing and following Christ, many of them decided to stay. However they had brought only enough provisions for a short visit. Thousands of them were in town with a new, vibrant faith in Jesus

Christ, but without money or credit cards. Barnabas didn't just note the situation and say, "What a shame!" He did something about it. He "sold a field he owned and brought the money and put it at the apostles' feet" (Acts 4:36). His act of radical generosity encouraged the new church.

We don't usually give ourselves nicknames. George, the misfit character in the comedy show *Seinfeld,* tried that, but his efforts backfired. In his quest for a new image he ordered a T-bone steak at every restaurant, and he tried hard to convince his peers to call him "T-bone." Instead he ended up with the nickname Koko because he reminded his coworkers of the famous gorilla.

More often, nicknames originate when others notice something distinctive about us. I know all about that. When I was a boy, my family called me Chocolate (pronounced cho-co-LAH-tay in Spanish) because of my love for sweets and chocolate. I didn't go around campaigning for the name; my family gave it to me. You see, a nickname says something about the person. The nickname Chocolate means I like sweets. I might have preferred "mighty warrior," but that's okay. After all, it's a lot better than Koko (poor George).

What if you and I were given nicknames based on our character? Keeping in mind that *bar* means *son,* some of us would be called Bar-complainer, Bar-gossiper, Bar-passive, Bar-liar, or Bar-controller. Others would be known as Bar-joy, Bar-hope, Bar-peace, Bar-love . . . or maybe Bar-encouragement, Barnabas.

People don't often appreciate encouragement when things are going well, but they cling to it like a life raft in times of trouble. Barnabas appears in Luke's narrative when people were in need. When new believers had financial concerns, Barnabas stepped up and gave generously. When Saul was an outcast, Barnabas acknowledged his potential instead of considering him a threat. We often despise suffering and persecution, but it's during those times when we are more receptive to encouragement . . . from the Holy Spirit and from people who are filled with the Spirit.

POWERFUL PARTNERS

In the persecution following Stephen's execution, believers fled as far as the coastland of Phoenicia (modern Lebanon), the island of Cyprus, and Antioch. The third most important city in the Roman Empire, Antioch was located at the northeast corner of the Mediterranean Sea. When Philip traveled to that area, he preached the gospel to the Jews. Some of them believed and began to tell the Gentiles about Jesus, and many of *them* believed. This was an amazing event. Historically, Jews and Gentiles despised each other. Now they were praising God with one voice. It was like a church with blacks, Latinos, and whites; rich and poor; immigrants and natives—all with the same heart for God.

When the news of this marvelous event reached Jerusalem, the apostles sent Barnabas to Antioch to help those believers grow in their faith in God and their love for one another. He made an impact, encouraging them, and drawing even more people to faith in Christ.

And while he was in that part of the world, Barnabas took on an additional mission. He went to nearby Tarsus to find Saul, who may have been in Tarsus for as long as ten years. Barnabas located him and brought him back to Antioch. Barnabas knew that to be an encourager often involves sacrifice. He didn't wait for Saul to come to him. In those days, travel was difficult and dangerous, but Barnabas didn't care. He left the comfort of a growing ministry to find one person, one man who would take the gospel to the farthest reaches of civilization.

For a year, those two unlikely partners—the generous encourager and the converted oppressor—oversaw the church, taught the Word, and led even more people to Jesus. It was in Antioch that believers were first called Christians. The unbelievers in Antioch may have intended the term as a derogatory slur—it means "little messiahs" or "belonging to Christ"—but the believers wore it as a badge of honor.

Later, as prophets in Antioch were praying and fasting, the Holy Spirit told them, "Set apart for me Barnabas and Saul for the work to which I have called them" (Acts 13:2). They prayed for the two men and sent them off on their first missionary journey to preach the gospel and plant churches in areas that had no knowledge of Jesus Christ. Theirs was a powerful partnership.

At first, Barnabas was the prominent partner. He took the initiative and taught Saul, whose mission from God was to take the gospel to the Gentiles. Perhaps that was why he stopped using his Jewish name, Saul, and began using a Greek or Roman name, Paul.

Before long, however, Paul's preaching and leadership gifts became evident to all. He became the leader in the partnership. When their roles shifted, Barnabas wasn't jealous or petty. He gladly yielded the platform to Paul. He was generous with his money, with his time, and with the mission God had given them.

When others doubted Paul had become a believer, Barnabas saw his potential. When Paul spent a long time alone in Tarsus, Barnabas left a thriving ministry to find him and get him involved. When normal jockeying for prestige might have ruined a beautiful relationship, Barnabas gladly took a backseat and watched God work through Paul.

I don't think it's too much to say that without Barnabas, the believers in Jerusalem wouldn't have accepted Paul. Without Barnabas, Paul would have languished in Tarsus. Without Barnabas, Paul wouldn't have become one of the greatest leaders in church history. Without Barnabas, Paul wouldn't have contributed such rich letters and inspiring theology to the New Testament.

Barnabas also saw potential in another young leader—John Mark. After the young man abandoned Paul and Barnabas on one of their missionary journeys, Paul gave up on him, but Barnabas was more patient and forgiving. John Mark later wrote the Gospel of Mark (and redeemed himself in Paul's eyes), so Barnabas had his thumbprint on another major portion of the Scriptures. No matter where he went, Barnabas had the God-given ability to look past obvious flaws in people to see enormous potential.

LOOKING FOR BARNABAS TODAY

We need people like Barnabas in the church today. We need people who see beyond a teenager's dark, angry glare and detect a sensitive, tender heart. We need people to come alongside an insecure introvert or an angry abuser and see a beautiful person waiting to be revealed. We need people to get beyond a couple's fierce arguments to help them uncover the love that has been buried far too long. We need people to see the potential of broken, resentful, addicted men and women, boys and girls. Most of us turn from such people. We don't want to get involved in their messy lives, and we don't want our good reputations to be tarnished by their bad ones. But Barnabas didn't live in fear of his reputation. He was willing to look beyond the obvious and beneath the surface. Other people were terrified of Paul; Barnabas saw the latent leadership strengths and repentant heart of a humbled man.

If we're looking for a church full of perfect people, we're going to be disappointed. The church is made up of people who are messed up, but they're honest enough to realize they need help—God's amazing love, forgiveness, and acceptance.

The church is made up of people who are messed up, but they're honest enough to realize they need help—God's amazing love, forgiveness, and acceptance.

In *The Reason for God,* pastor and author Tim Keller observed:

> "I realize that so many people's main problem with Christianity has far more to do with the church than with Jesus. They don't want to be told that to become a Christian and live a Christian life they need to find a church they can thrive in. They've had too many bad experiences with churches. I fully understand. I will grant that, on the whole, churchgoers may be weaker psychologically and morally than non-churchgoers. That should be no more surprising than the fact that people sitting in a doctor's office are on the whole sicker than those who are not there. Churches rightly draw a higher proportion of needy people. They also have a great number of people whose lives have been completely turned around and filled by the joy of Christ."[23]

We may be messed up in our marriages, with our children, in our jobs and our finances, in our destructive addictions, and in our annoying habits, but we're trusting God to cleanse us and change us from the inside out.

Barnabas wasn't looking for an easy life. He wanted a life that counted, so he was willing to sell his property to help people he didn't even know. He wasn't looking for a comfortable life. He trusted God to give him eyes to see into the heart of a murderer and impart life and hope. Like no one else, Barnabas realized Paul's angry passion could be molded by grace into a tenacious faith to fulfill God's calling.

I heard a story of a man who got excited when he heard a sermon about the importance of sacrificial service. He made an appointment to see the pastor, and he told him, "Pastor, I'm here to get personally involved by using all my gifts in a ministry of sensitivity and extreme sacrifice to challenge a secularized, value-impoverished society with the radical claims of the gospel of Jesus Christ."

"Great," the pastor says. "When can you start?"

"I have Thursday afternoons free from 3:00 to 4:00."

The man, like many of us, was clueless about the cost of following Christ and the price necessary when investing our time, talents, and treasure to encourage people in need. For Barnabas—and for us—the price is high, but it's how God uses us to radically change lives with His love, His power, and His wisdom.

We often romanticize the early church and say, "Man, I wish we could go back to the way things were in Acts." Yeah, right.

Those believers were arrested and tortured, run out of town and persecuted. And when they got together, they argued about whether Gentiles (which includes most of the people reading this book) could possibly be accepted by God! With that suspicion and deep-seated hatred, you can imagine the quality of their relationships.

It was in this environment that God used Barnabas like a beacon of light. Barnabas realized the love and power of God could transform individuals so they could reach out to accept those who had been their enemies. Pagans and Jews, outsiders and insiders, all are welcome in the family of God. But it took a special man to stand in the expanding gap—for Paul, for the church, and for every generation after them that has benefited from Barnabas's ability to see potential where others resisted.

Sometimes, finding potential in people isn't easy. They may not be simply *different*; they may seem genuinely unlovable. Mother Teresa is known for her care for the poorest people in India. Her compassion, however, was born from tragedy. When she was eight years old, her father died mysteriously. In her pain, she reached out for comfort from two sources: her mother and her God. Her mother was a generous, gracious woman. Though she wasn't wealthy, she often invited poor people in their city of Macedonia to come for dinner. Young Teresa was paying attention.

Teresa attended a school run by a convent, and when she was old enough, she took holy orders. Her apprenticeship was in India. She was assigned to a school to teach geography and history to the poorest children in Calcutta. About a decade later, while she was on a train to a retreat in the mountains, she heard the voice of Jesus: "I want Indian Nuns, Missionaries of Charity, who would be My fire of love amongst the poor, the sick, the dying, and the little children. I know you are the most incapable person—weak and sinful but just because you are that—I want to use you for My glory. Wilt thou refuse?"

With no more than a vague sense of direction, Mother Teresa crafted a plan and took action to educate, feed, and nurture Calcutta's poor. She began a school and opened a home for the dying who had nowhere else to go. Her work, which had only twelve members at the time, soon expanded to include a leper colony, a nursing home, an orphanage, and many mobile health clinics.

By the time she died in 1997, her charity numbered over 4,000 staff members and many thousands of volunteers, with 610 foundations in 123 countries. Mother Teresa was a woman of great faith, but few words. Her compassion for outcasts spoke volumes about her heart and her tenacity to care for those our society has discarded. She once observed, "We think sometimes that poverty is only being hungry, naked, and homeless. The poverty of being unwanted, unloved, and uncared for is the greatest poverty. We must start in our own homes to remedy this kind of poverty."[24]

> The poverty of being unwanted, unloved, and uncared for is the greatest poverty.

Like Mother Teresa, will you look beyond the color of a person's skin and see a heart that can be melted and molded by the love of Jesus?

Will you look past a person's accent or language to befriend someone from a different culture?

Will you care so much about another person's tragic circumstances that you don't care what others think of you as you reach out?

Will you think more of God's calling to love people than the pleasure of finding fault with those who disagree with your politics?

Will you sacrifice comfort to care for those in need?

Will you set aside your agenda to get on God's agenda to love "the least of these"?

It's ironic that in the same chapter that tells how God sent Barnabas to Antioch to bring pagan and Jewish believers together, the Spirit gave Peter a vision and told him, "Do not call anything impure that God has made clean" (Acts 11:9). One of the marks of a self-righteous church is to establish dividing lines between this kind of person and that one, this ethnic group and that one, this political persuasion and that one. Like Peter, Barnabas must have been listening to the Spirit, because he refused to call unclean his partner Paul or the Gentiles, who were traditionally despised by the Jews.

The impact of Barnabas on Paul is a very personal message for me. When I was sixteen years old, I was a knucklehead. To say the least, I was raw. Like many adolescents, I was struggling to find my way. I had grown up in a tough neighborhood, and I had never heard the message of God's grace until some young people in a Pentecostal church loved me and told me about Jesus. The gospel seemed almost too good to be true! I joined the church, and I wanted to grow. I wanted God to use me to touch others' lives.

One day in church, a woman walked up to me. I guess she thought she was making a prophetic announcement when she looked into my eyes and said, "Young man, you're never going to amount to anything!" I was crushed. But somehow, I knew better than to listen to her. Her message was the opposite of the Good News. Hers was really bad news! She was the anti-Barnabas.

I pushed her message out of my mind and heart. It wasn't easy, but it was essential. If I had listened to her, I wouldn't have continued to pursue Jesus. I would have given up in despair. I wouldn't have believed God could ever use me to plant churches, build leaders, and establish the Chicago Dream Center to turn people's lives around with the power of God's grace. If I had believed her, I would have vanished in the backwater world of poverty and hopelessness. But thank God, He brought some people like Barnabas into my life. That woman didn't see any potential in the raw material of my life, but they did. They weren't blind. They realized I was a knucklehead, but they loved me anyway—and they believed God had a purpose for me. I fed off their faith . . . in God and in me. My life is different today because God gave me a Barnabas or two to encourage me when I had little faith in my future.

Now I want to be a Barnabas in the lives of the people around me. God put a young lady in our lives thirteen years ago, and we were happy to welcome her as part of the family. Yolanda was born in El Salvador before the years of civil unrest of the 1980s and '90s. Her father abandoned the family when she was only six years old. All she had was her mom and two brothers. Things took a turn for the worse when she was eight years old. Her mother was shot and killed—likely as a result of the political instability in the country. The cloud of mystery surrounding her mother's death added to Yolanda's grief and sadness.

After her mother died, she lived with her father for a while, and then with other relatives. She was constantly moving; any semblance of family stability was gone. When she was twelve, she moved to the United States with her father and brothers. At last they were together as a family, and the restoration process began.

In America, Yolanda began visiting the church her grandparents attended. There, she heard the message of the gospel and received Jesus as her Savior. For the first time since she was a little girl, she began to feel hope for the future. All through high school, she pursued God with the help of her church family. After graduation she attended an Assemblies of God Christian College, and there felt called by God to serve in ministry.

She came to our church thirteen years ago—right after she graduated from college with dreams of ministry in her heart. For years she served faithfully, overcame her past, and grew in grace. As she served, God restored her relationship with her father and family members. She was even given the opportunity to serve as a missionary in her native country of El Salvador. For Yolanda, it was a dream come true. Today she serves as an assistant in Spanish ministry and with a team that reaches out to victims of sex trafficking.

In a moment of reflection and tenderness, Yolanda told me that I have been the only consistent father figure she has ever known. Recently, her father passed away. I told her that when she gets married, I would like the honor of walking her down the aisle.

When we make a commitment to encourage people, to see their potential even when they see none, we pay a price. They may not believe our positive message because they've been hurt so deeply and for so long. The past—either their sins or the wounds created by others' sins, or both—may haunt them and shackle them to bitterness and self-pity. They expect people to condemn them. They expect people to abandon them.

They expect people to give up on them. But we refuse to give up. Gradually, our encouragement erodes the walls of self-doubt and discouragement. A door to the heart cracks open and lets in some love. Then, amazing things can happen!

THE SOURCE

The kind of encouragement demonstrated by Barnabas is far more than a passing compliment or a friendly smile. It's a tenacious love, a persistent optimism, and a steadfast faith that God can work wonders to turn people's lives around. But it's not foolish, blind, or naïve. Barnabas had spiritual eyes that saw the potential in Paul, and he was willing to risk his own reputation and comfort to pour himself into a man who was feared by some and despised by others.

Barnabas is the only person in the book of Acts described as a "good man." Luke tells us, "He was a good man, full of the Holy Spirit and faith, and a great number of people were brought to the Lord" (Acts 11:24). A good man is one who is amazed at God's grace, so he is both humble and bold. He trusts in Christ's righteousness, not his own. He has courage to obey God's directives even when it's inconvenient to do so, even when he may look foolish to

> The kind of encouragement demonstrated by Barnabas is far more than a passing compliment or a friendly smile. It's a tenacious love.

others, even at the expense of his life. It's a person who is filled with the Spirit of God instead of being tied to a personal agenda.

Where do we find the heart to reach out to those who are different from us? We love because we've experienced God's amazing love for us. John wrote, "This is love: not that we loved God, but that he loved us and sent his Son as an atoning sacrifice for our sins. Dear friends, since God so loved us, we also ought to love one another" (1 John 4:10–11).

We forgive because we draw from the deep well of God's forgiveness of our own sins. Paul described it: "Therefore, as God's chosen people, holy and dearly loved, clothe yourselves with compassion, kindness, humility, gentleness and patience. Bear with each other and forgive one another if any of you has a grievance against someone. Forgive as the Lord forgave you" (Col. 3:12–13).

And we accept people because we are overwhelmed with Jesus' warm embrace. Paul told us, "Accept one another, then, just as Christ accepted you, in order to bring praise to God" (Rom. 15:7).

Wouldn't you love to have a friend like Barnabas? Wouldn't the people in your family, in your business, in your church, and in your neighborhood love for you to be like him? They're waiting for you to step into their pain with the healing salve of God's love instead of condemnation. They're waiting for you to understand that their defensiveness is a reaction to their deep pain, so you will love them even when they're "touchy." They're waiting for you to speak words of life and hope instead of criticism.

Husbands and wives have the opportunity to be like Barnabas with one another. Parents have the opportunity to be like Barnabas to their children. Friends have the opportunity to be like Barnabas to each other.

If you'll make a commitment to be a Barnabas in others' lives, God will bring a Barnabas or two into your life. It's the law of the harvest: we reap what we sow. What are you sowing?

Barnabas stood in the gap for Paul when no one believed in him and no one wanted him. There are people around you today in the same condition. Be like Barnabas. Dig deep to experience the love, forgiveness, and acceptance of Christ, and then let His grace overflow from your heart into the lives of those around you. Uncover their potential. They'll never be the same. Neither will you.

THINK ABOUT IT . . .

1. After Saul's conversion, if you had been a nonbelieving Jew hearing him preach about Jesus, how would you have responded to him? If you had been a Christian and had seen the change in him, how would you have responded?

2. What does it truly mean to encourage people? How does it affect them?

3. What are some costs we might incur when we pour ourselves into others' lives?

4. Why is it important to avoid being naïve and foolish when we relate to people whose lives are a wreck? How can we become more perceptive, more hopeful, and more courageous?

5. What are some excuses people make to avoid the cost of investing time, talent, and treasure into hurting, struggling people?

6. If those who know you gave you a nickname, like Bar-whatever, what would it be? What do you want it to be?

7. Why is it crucial to experience Christ's love, forgiveness, and acceptance so deeply that it overflows from us? What happens when we try to help people but we aren't filled with the Spirit?

8. Has God put anyone on your heart as you've read this chapter? What's your next step?

9. What is God saying to you through the story of Barnabas?

6 JOHN THE BAPTIST

. . . was willing to take risks

"From the days of John the Baptist until now, the kingdom of heaven has been subjected to violence, and violent people have been raiding it. For all the Prophets and the Law prophesied until John. And if you are willing to accept it, he is the Elijah who was to come. He who has ears, let him hear" (Matt. 11:12–15).

People who stand in the gap for others don't come from a standard one-size-fits-all mold. They're different . . . really different. We've looked at Nehemiah, a gifted and compassionate government employee; Esther, a beautiful queen: Noah, a man who prepared his family for a catastrophe; David, an overlooked shepherd boy; and Barnabas, a man who was a mentor's mentor. They were very different people with different circumstances, but the calling of God was the same: to listen to His voice and stand in the gap in times of weakness, vulnerability, and danger. In this chapter we're going to look at one of the strangest people in the Bible, John the Baptist. If you've been thinking you don't fit the mold of a "gap person," keep reading. John is your guy.

FLASHBACK

The last of the Old Testament books was written about 400 years before the birth of Jesus. During the interim, it seemed God was silent. For generation after generation, God's people waited for the promised Messiah to come to free them. Some people became impatient and fought bloody wars against the Syrians and Roman occupying forces. When the Roman legions took control, the Jews longed even more for the Messiah to appear. But first, they had been told, another man would come to announce His coming.

That other man was John the Baptist. When we get our first description of him, he seems like a throwback to the ancient prophets, a character straight out of the pages of the Old Testament. But John wasn't an incidental character in God's story to save the world. In fact, John's role had been predicted by the prophets hundreds of years before, and Luke opens his Gospel with a long account of John's birth. If Oscars had been awarded in the salvation story, John would have won for Best Actor in a Supporting Role.

The angel Gabriel appeared to John's father, Zechariah, and told the old man that he would have a son. The angel said:

> "Do not be afraid, Zechariah; your prayer has been heard. Your wife Elizabeth will bear you a son, and you are to call him John. He will be a joy and delight to you, and many will rejoice because of his birth, for he will be

> great in the sight of the Lord. He is never to take wine or other fermented drink, and he will be filled with the Holy Spirit even before he is born. He will bring back many of the people of Israel to the Lord their God. And he will go on before the Lord, in the spirit and power of Elijah, to turn the hearts of the parents to their children and the disobedient to the wisdom of the righteous—to make ready a people prepared for the Lord" (Luke 1:13–17).

Elijah was one of the most famous and powerful prophets in the Bible. It had been predicted that Elijah would come to announce the coming of the Messiah. Gabriel told John's dumbfounded dad that his baby boy would come "in the spirit and power of Elijah"! And that's not all. Gabriel said John would turn the hearts of fathers to their children.

We may not raise our eyebrows when we read this, but any Jew in the first century would instantly realize that those words appear in the very last verse of the very last line of Malachi, the very last book of the Old Testament. John would be the bridge between the old and the new, the promise and its fulfillment, the anticipation of the Messiah and His arrival—the answer to all their hopes.

I can imagine the conversations Zechariah had with John when he was a boy. "Son, I know you want to skip school, but remember, you're in training. In a few years you'll prepare the world for God's King. And by the way, eat your beans. You need to stay strong." John grew up knowing he had a special calling. He played a crucial role in the most important event in the history of the world.

PREPARE THE WAY

John's job was to get people ready for Jesus. He called them to repent: to take stock of their lives, realize they were sinners, and turn to God. Repentance is a message of change. It's a response to God's searing light shining on our deepest sins, and then humbly acknowledging that we need His forgiveness. True repentance isn't just internal; a changed heart becomes evident in changed attitudes and actions.

True repentance isn't just internal; a changed heart becomes evident in changed attitudes and actions.

Repentance is a message of good news and bad news, but the bad news comes first: "You're a sinner, hopelessly lost without God's love and grace." Then the good news: "But God loves you, forgives you, and will radically change your heart and your destiny if you'll let Him."

John welcomed anyone whose heart was humble, anyone who was willing to repent and be baptized. But his baptism pointed to something bigger and better. He told those who questioned him, "I baptize with water, but among you stands one you do not know. He is the one who comes after me, the straps of whose sandals I am not worthy to untie" (John 1:26). The water of John's baptism pointed to the blood of Jesus Christ.

John obviously hadn't read any books on winning friends, and he didn't go to charm school. Matthew describes him this way:

> "In those days John the Baptist came, preaching in the Desert of Judea and saying, 'Repent, for the kingdom of heaven has come near.' This is he who was spoken of through the prophet Isaiah: 'A voice of one calling in the wilderness, "Prepare the way for the Lord, make straight paths for him."' John's clothes were made of camel's hair, and he had a leather belt around his waist. His food was locusts and wild honey" (Matt. 3:1–4).

How would you like this guy to sit next to you on the bus, in school, in the office, or in church? He smelled, he wore weird clothes, and his diet was either innovative or just plain weird. His message, though simple and profound, could be as off-putting as his appearance. Unlike many modern preachers, he didn't sugarcoat his words, and he wasn't interested in entertaining the crowd. People came to him from the whole region, and he baptized them in the Jordan River. But when the religious leaders showed up, he told them,

> "You brood of vipers! Who warned you to flee from the coming wrath? Produce fruit in keeping with repentance. And do not think you can say to yourselves, 'We have Abraham as our father.' I tell you that out of these stones God can raise up children for Abraham. The ax is already at the root of the trees, and every tree that does not produce good fruit will be cut down and thrown into the fire" (Matt. 3:7–10).

John was drawing a line in the sand—a different line than people were used to. Most people assumed the religious leaders had an inside track with God and that everyone else, the normal sinners, were outsiders. John turned that thinking upside down. Imagine being one of the religious leaders blasted by John at the riverbank. They were furious! But imagine being a regular person who had been afraid of the condemnation of the religious elite. You would think, *Wow! John is amazing! Maybe God has something for me after all!*

John didn't treat people the way the religious leaders did. He didn't make class distinctions. He didn't show preference to the rich and powerful over the poor and powerless. He called *all* people to repent, to turn from sin to God's forgiveness, to change from their selfishness to care about the things God cares about. Some people may have traveled to the Jordan just for the show. They couldn't find anything like John in their hometowns! But many came because he offered hope—hope at last for a level playing field of faith, and even more, hope that the Messiah was coming soon. He was finally coming!

If John came to your house and sat down for coffee at your breakfast table, what do you think he would say to you? Do you think he would apologize for tracking mud from his sandals on the floor? Probably not. Would he engage in small talk: "Hey, what did you think of the game last night?" or "Nice granite counters. Where'd you get them? Did you get a good deal?" No, he wouldn't even notice. He would lean forward, look into your eyes, and ask, "Tell me, how's your soul? Are you close to God? Are you doing what God has called you to do? No excuses . . . no retreats. What has God told you to do that you haven't done yet? What are you waiting for? It's time, you know." You wouldn't get the idea that John enjoyed blasting people. He delighted in seeing people love God with all their hearts. Nothing less. That was his commitment, and he expected the same from others.

Repentance always leads to noticeable changes in behavior. When people came to the river to hear John and be baptized, he told them, "Produce fruit in keeping with repentance" (Luke 3:8). He realized that when people are called to change their behavior, the excuses start flying! The Jews often insisted they didn't need to change because they were Abraham's children. That, they were sure, was their protection. John didn't buy their excuse (Luke 3:8–9).

The people felt nailed to the wall by John's honesty and integrity. They wanted to know, "What should we do then?"

John didn't give them vague generalities like "be nice" or "play well with others." He listed specific acts of repentance for each kind of person present:

> "John answered, 'Anyone who has two shirts should share with the one who has none, and anyone who has food should do the same.'
>
> Even tax collectors came to be baptized. 'Teacher,' they asked, 'what should we do?'
>
> 'Don't collect any more than you are required to,' he told them.
>
> Then some soldiers asked him, 'And what should we do?'
>
> He replied, 'Don't extort money and don't accuse people falsely—be content with your pay'" (Luke 3:11–14).

Accepting the bad news about sin, though, is essential if we're going to embrace the good news of God's forgiveness—transformation requires both.

The message of change challenged people then, and it still challenges us today. It's much easier just to go along to get along, to be passive, to avoid making waves, and to take things as they are. Accepting the bad news about sin, though, is essential if we're going to embrace the good news of God's forgiveness—transformation requires both. We may go in the wrong direction for a long time: drugs, alcohol, illicit sex, greed, bitterness, self-pity, and a hundred other self-destructive, self-absorbed behaviors. Then one day we hear a song or listen to a message, and the lights come on in our hearts. We confess our sins to God and experience His cleansing flood. Our insides are changed, and our outsides are changed, too . . . and people notice. They wonder, "What's up with her?" "What's going on with him?" "The person I knew is radically different!" That's repentance.

John stood in the 400-year gap between the Old and the New Testaments. To understand the hurts and hopes of the Jewish people in the first century, we need to go all the way back to Solomon's temple. At the dedication ceremony, the glory of God filled the temple in a way that was astounding and overwhelming. Surely, people thought, God's presence would be with them in the temple forever.

Yet a few centuries later, as we saw in the narrative about Nehemiah, God's people turned their backs on God. The northern kingdom of Israel fell to the Assyrians, and later the southern kingdom of Judah fell to the Babylonians. Jerusalem and the temple were in Judah. The Babylonians plundered God's temple, stole all the gold, and tore the building to the ground.

This loss was much more than a few possessions. The spiritual heart of the Jewish nation was ripped out.

Ezekiel tells us that God's presence departed from the temple before the Babylonians attacked (Ezek. 10). After Zerubbabel and Ezra rebuilt the temple in about 515 BC, the people expected God's glory to fill the temple again, but He didn't come. They weren't just waiting; they were waiting in the dark of disappointment and confusion. Had God abandoned them forever?

During those centuries, God's people suffered, waited, and hoped their King would come in glory to the temple again. But when He came, hardly anyone noticed. When Mary and Joseph took the baby Jesus to the temple to be dedicated, we are told of only two elderly people, Simeon and Anna, who were there to witness the event. God's glory had come back, but not in the way anyone expected.

About thirty years later, when Jesus appeared at the Jordan River, it was John's supreme moment. It was everything he had prepared for. He announced to the crowd, "Look, the Lamb of God, who takes away the sin of the world! This is the one I meant when I said, 'A man who comes after me has surpassed me because he was before me'" (John 1:29–30). To confirm to everyone at the river that day that Jesus was the Messiah, God sent the Spirit like a dove to descend on Him. John then baptized Jesus, not because Jesus needed forgiveness, but to launch

His ministry. From that moment on, Jesus the King marched toward the cross and the establishment of His kingdom.

John's message was that the King had come, not as a great warrior with a flaming sword on a mighty horse, but as a carpenter's son. The King would someday come with the angels in power and might, but John introduced Him as "the Lamb of God who takes away the sins of the world." It was John's incredible privilege to herald the King's unexpected appearance. God hadn't spoken for 400 years. To break the long, intense silence, He chose an intense guy wearing strange clothes with a crystal clear message. He chose John to call people to repent, be baptized, and look to Jesus.

Four hundred years is a long, long time. When we have to wait, we may turn to other sources for hope and comfort. Many people turn to the government to solve their problems, others turn to drugs or money or violence to get what they want. Some numb their emptiness by trying to fill it with television, sports, shopping, or food. John reminds us that there is only one true King, only one genuine Savior, only one hope for the world. Look to Jesus. He may seem slow to appear, but He's always on time.

DECLARE THE WAY

We might read the accounts about John the Baptist and conclude, "That John was one of a kind. I'm sure glad God no longer expects us to be like that!" Not so fast. No, God hasn't told us to wear camel skins and eat locusts and honey, but He has called us to wear something that may look just as strange to the people in our culture. God has told us to clothe ourselves in righteousness, justice, and mercy. We put on honesty and integrity instead of lying and cutting corners. We put on marital fidelity instead of sexual impurity. We put on generosity instead of greed. We put on forgiveness and mercy instead of arrogance, self-pity, and bitterness. When that is how we clothe ourselves, we look just as weird to the people in our culture as John did in his.

The Scriptures don't say much about John's circle of friends, but I can imagine that he didn't mingle easily. He wasn't skilled at small talk. But the friends he had were dear ones who trusted him completely. Similarly, when we clothe ourselves with righteousness, justice, and mercy, we shouldn't be surprised when plenty of people don't understand us—or worse, resist our love and condemn us for our attempts to point them to Jesus. But as we live in grace and truth, we'll find the best friends we've ever known.

Responses to John the Baptist and Jesus were not mild. Both men were dividing lines, forks in the road for every person they met. They challenged passivity and self-absorption, and they pointed people to a life of meaning and risk. For every person who responded positively, many more found the challenge to be offensive. Similarly, a few people will join us in following God with all our hearts, but many others will think we've lost our minds. That's okay. They said the same thing about John and Jesus.

A few people will join us in following God with all our hearts, but many others will think we've lost our minds.

As we follow John's example, we will find our voice to speak out about Jesus. We won't mind if people think more of Him than they do of us. In fact, we will be thrilled to take second place. One part of our message is that Jesus is coming back. John was the forerunner when Jesus came the first time. He announced His coming. We are the forerunners of the second coming of Jesus Christ. We have the indescribable privilege of announcing to everyone who will listen that He's coming back to establish His kingdom!

Like John, we can be the voice of God to our families and communities. As our hearts are soaked in the truth of God's Word, we will be like sponges that are squeezed and flowing with the truth and grace we have absorbed.

Other times the voices we hear won't be full of grace and truth. Even in places where we expect God's love and strength to flow, we can be exposed to negative messages. It happened to me in the church after I became a Christian, and it can happen to anyone. People may wear nice smiles when they walk through the church doors on Sunday morning, but we are unaware of the anguish and anger they may feel. We don't hear the soul-killing words spoken at home—and even in the car before they get out, put on their smiles, and come in to worship. We live in a world of powerful and mixed messages, so we need to be shrewd, objective, and observant about the things we hear.

John's father was a respected spiritual leader. Zechariah was a priest who led people in worship and taught the Scriptures in the temple. He and his wife Elizabeth hadn't been able to have any children. One day as he performed his duties, the angel Gabriel appeared and told him that their prayers were answered: God was going to give them a son. This son, to be named John, had a special calling. He was the long predicted forerunner of the Messiah.

You would think that the appearance of one of the two top angels in the universe would convince a person, but it wasn't enough for Zechariah. He doubted Gabriel and his promise. To keep the old priest from poisoning the family with doubt and negative words, the angel made Zechariah mute for the entire term of Elizabeth's pregnancy. Gabriel, God's mouthpiece, was saying, "Zechariah, I don't care what your position is in the temple. I can't have you abort God's purpose with your fears and doubts. I'm going to make sure your voice can't stop what God wants to do, so you won't be able to speak until you see the promise of John's birth fulfilled."

Some of us wish Gabriel would appear in our homes to make a husband, wife, teenager, child, or parents mute for nine months! That's not the point. The issue is that negative, poisonous, deflating messages can come from anywhere. Many people use criticism as clubs to beat people up, and they use pessimism to drag others down to their level. We need to reject such messages—especially if they're coming from our own lips!

Zechariah must have learned his lesson, because under his care, John became a mighty man of God with a powerfully positive message: Get ready. The King is coming!

Our message about Jesus is just as revolutionary as John's at the riverside. The world screams that we can't be happy unless we have this product or that experience. It promises that beauty, riches, pleasure, and popularity will fill our hearts and provide all we ever wanted. Every magazine ad, every television commercial, and every billboard along the highway shouts this message—explicitly or implicitly. To some degree, they're all lies. They promise something they can't deliver.

In stark contrast, our message is that our only hope is found in the sacrificial death of the Son of God. The gospel of grace humbles us to the dust because we realize we're sinners who are desperately lost without Christ—no matter how much beauty, wealth, pleasure, and popularity we have. The love and acceptance of God's grace, though, doesn't leave us in the dust. It raises us to the stars with full hearts and a new purpose. Our names are engraved on the palms of God's hands (Isa. 49:16). We are a chosen race, a holy nation, a people belonging to God (1 Peter 2:9–10). And our message is to invite others to experience His kindness and strength, grace and glory, love and power. Only then can we love those who hate us, rejoice in tribulation, give generously without expecting anything in return, and pour ourselves out in sacrificial service to God and to our neighbors. This is a categorically opposite message from the ads in magazines, on television, and the billboards we pass each day. We need to notice the difference. Experiencing the love of God comforts us in our pain and puts steel in our souls. It will make us heroes.

Experiencing the love of God comforts us in our pain and puts steel in our souls. It will make us heroes.

In the spring of 1940, the German war machine stormed past the defenses of France, Belgium, Denmark, and Holland to conquer much of Western Europe. Shockingly, it was all over in a few weeks, and Hitler received France's surrender in Paris. The Nazis had been persecuting Jews for years in Germany and Austria. Now, Jewish people in those countries were in danger. Some noble Gentiles risked their lives to save a few of them. In Amsterdam, Corrie ten Boom's parents believed the Jews were God's chosen people, so they readily agreed to hide a woman who asked for help. Soon, other Jews showed up at their door asking to be hidden from the Nazi Gestapo.

Corrie's family kept endangered Jews in "the hiding place" for almost two years until a Dutch informant told the Nazis about them. The whole family was arrested. Corrie's father died only days later. Soon, Corrie and her sister Betsie were sent to Ravensbruck concentration camp where they suffered severe hardships, cold, and countless indignities. Betsie died a few days before a clerical error allowed Corrie to be freed. Before she died, Betsie told her sister, "There is no pit so deep that [God] is not deeper still."

When she was released, Corrie wanted God to use her suffering for His glory. She wrote *The Hiding Place* and helped to establish a rehabilitation center in the Netherlands. With the same combination of humility and tenacity displayed by John the Baptist, Corrie explained her motivation to live for Christ:

> "Do you know what hurts so very much? It's love. Love is the strongest force in the world, and when it is blocked that means pain. There are two things we can do when this happens. We can kill that love so that it stops hurting. But then of course part of us dies, too. Or we can ask God to open up another route for that love to travel."[25]

Like Corrie, John knew "another route" was the love, grace, and power of Jesus Christ.

GET OUT OF THE WAY

John's assignment had a limited timeframe. In most organizations, people expect to climb the corporate ladder and achieve higher positions and salaries. In the kingdom, it's different. John's role was to point people to Jesus, and then get out of the way. He had been preaching that another was coming, someone far more important than himself. It was his great privilege and high honor to baptize Jesus and launch the greatest mission the world has ever known.

At that moment, many of us would have a hard time backing out of the spotlight to let someone else take center stage, but John didn't have a hint of jealousy or regret. In fact, he had been living for this exchange. When someone complained to John that Jesus was becoming more popular than him, he replied,

> "A person can receive only what is given them from heaven. You yourselves can testify that I said, 'I am not the Messiah but am sent ahead of him.' The bride belongs to the bridegroom. The friend who attends the bridegroom waits and listens for him, and is full of joy when he hears the bridegroom's voice. That joy is mine, and it is now complete. He must become greater; I must become less" (John 3:27–30).

Instead of jealousy, John felt genuine joy to see crowds of people flock to Jesus. John didn't care about his prestige, his status, or his role. He only cared about fulfilling the task God had given him to announce the coming of the King.

That's our assignment, too. It is our privilege and honor to tell people about Jesus, that He is the mighty King and the suffering Servant, the Lion and the Lamb, the hope of the world. It's easy for us to get off message. When we talk to our family or neighbors, we often tell them about our church or our pastor or the great music or the children's ministry. It's wonderful to appreciate those things, but they matter only because (and if) they point people to Jesus! Don't get off track. Talk about Jesus, who He is, why He died, and how He has changed your life. Remind people that Jesus is their hope for meaning now and for a glorious future when He returns to establish His kingdom on earth.

Don't get off track. Talk about Jesus, who He is, why He died, and how He has changed your life.

John saw himself as the best man at the wedding feast of the Lamb. The best man knows he's not the center of attention. He's thrilled to shine a light on his friend, the groom, and tell all kinds of stories about him so everybody gets a glimpse of the groom's character and personality. At the rehearsal dinner and the reception, the best man stands up and speaks loudly and fondly of his friend. But when his speeches are over, he fades into the background. The groom and his bride are all that matter, and he's content with that. We get this picture when John makes his announcement about Jesus. I can see the grin on his face and hear the excitement in his voice as he yells for everyone to hear, "Look, the Lamb of God who takes away the sin of the world!"

John was the most popular preacher of his day. He could have had his own nationwide television show, and all the leading magazines and newspapers would have interviewed him. But none of that mattered to this humble man. He was content to be the best man, to point people to the groom and his bride, and then fade into the woodwork.

WE ALL NEED A REMINDER

We get one more glimpse of John about two years later. He hadn't stopped telling people about Jesus and calling people to repentance. This time, though, he had called Herod to repent of his adultery, and Herod wasn't very receptive to John's message. He threw John into prison, where John had lots of time to think about his life, his role, and his impending execution. In those days, the Jews were expecting their Messiah to come with military power to overthrow the Romans and reestablish the Davidic Kingdom. But Jesus had come as a humble servant, telling parables and healing people instead of leading an army of conquest. No wonder so many were confused or disappointed in Him! In the darkness of his prison cell, even John began to wonder. He sent his disciples to Jesus to ask, "Are you the one who is to come, or should we expect someone else?" (Matt. 11:3)

Jesus didn't react in anger. He didn't blame John for his doubts. He simply sent back a reply to reassure John and soothe his troubled mind: "Go back and report to John what you hear and see: The blind receive sight, the lame walk, those who have leprosy are cleansed, the deaf hear, the dead are raised, and the good news is proclaimed to the poor. Blessed is anyone who does not stumble on account of me" (Matt. 11:4–6).

How do we know Jesus wasn't upset with John? As soon as John's friends left with the words of assurance, Jesus turned to the crowd and told them,

"What did you go out into the wilderness to see? A reed swayed by the wind? If not, what did you go out to see? A man dressed in fine clothes? No, those who wear fine clothes are in kings' palaces. Then what did you go out to see? A prophet? Yes, I tell you, and more than a prophet. This is the one about whom it is written:

> 'I will send my messenger ahead of you, who will prepare your way before you.'
>
> Truly I tell you, among those born of women there has not risen anyone greater than John the Baptist; yet whoever is least in the kingdom of heaven is greater than he" (Matt. 11:7–11).

"No one greater than John the Baptist." What an affirmation from the mouth of the King! And yet someday, those of us who enter the new heaven and new earth in God's kingdom will be far more pure, strong, kind, faithful, and good.

Make no mistake: we're in a battle. Jesus explained, "From the days of John the Baptist until now, the kingdom of heaven has been subjected to violence, and violent people have been raiding it" (Matt. 11:12). The King and his people aren't passive. We are "forcefully advancing" to win souls from sin and death, transform families into havens of hope, and change communities into testimonies of God's greatness and goodness.

In Jesus' day, "forceful men" included Herod, who would soon have John's head on a platter, and the religious leaders who plotted to murder Jesus. Our fight today is often against enemies seen and unseen. Opponents try to tear us down and the government may pass laws that hurt our cause. Behind the scenes, invisible spiritual powers sow doubt and discouragement. Against such forces, we have to fight.

A few years later, Paul wrote,

> "Put on the full armor of God, so that you can take your stand against the devil's schemes. For our struggle is not against flesh and blood, but against the rulers, against the authorities, against the powers of this dark world and against the spiritual forces of evil in the heavenly realms. Therefore put on the full armor of God, so that

> when the day of evil comes, you may be able to stand your ground, and after you have done everything, to stand" (Eph. 6:11–13).

It's not enough to play at a commitment to Christ. It's not enough to drift in and out of church and hope something sticks. The task of every believer is to be like John—to stand in the gap in our generation to be a bridge between the old and the new. We call people to repentance, to turn from sin and doubt to faith in the Lamb of God. We face many obstacles and enemies, so we need to encourage each other to finish well. When doubts creep in—and they will—we need to go back to Jesus for reassurance.

Jennie needed more than reassurance; she desperately needed help. In fact, she had completely given up on life. As a child her family was so poor that they often picked through garbage in order to survive. Jennie's childhood was a nightmare. For years, she saw her father and mother verbally and physically abuse each other. The abuse, darkness, and misery were almost too much to take. She begged God to change her parents, but the chaos only got worse. At the young age of eleven, Jennie decided there must not be a God. She laughed at her friends who tried to convince her that God not only exists, but that He loved her. Jennie became what she called "an angry atheist."

She lived for fun, sex, and the thrill of being chased by men. A Christian friend tried to talk to her about God, but she didn't want to hear it. She was addicted to the party scene. By the time she was twenty-two, Jennie was the mother of a four-year-old boy, and pregnant again. She had abandoned her son and had decided there was no better option than to get an abortion to end her current pregnancy. Her boss even gave her $600 to pay for the abortion because he was convinced she was an unfit mother.

Jennie took the money and cried all the way to the clinic. The lady helping her fill out the paperwork reached her hand out from under the glass window and said, "Something tells me you don't want to do this. I'm going to reschedule you for next week."

The next day Jennie woke up thinking about suicide and decided she would hang herself in the bathroom. As she looked for something that would serve as a rope, her cell phone buzzed. She tried to turn it off, but turned it on instead. It was her Christian friend. Jennie explained what happened next: "I told her I couldn't live this life anymore and hung up on her. Within minutes she showed up at my apartment. I didn't answer when she knocked. She broke down my door and found me in the bathroom crying. She started talking to me about God, and I yelled at her and told her to get out. I screamed, 'Your god can't help me!' She told me, 'Please come to church with me tomorrow. If my God doesn't help you, then you can kill yourself.' I answered in an angry voice, 'I'll go, but when your God doesn't help me, I'll leave a suicide note letting the world know that there's no God.'"

The next day Jennie visited our church. We served Holy Communion that day, and my wife Elizabeth sang about Jesus dying on the cross. Jennie didn't understand the entire message of the song, but it reached deep inside her. She couldn't hold back her tears and began to sob. She wanted to run, but a gentle voice spoke, saying, "Welcome home." Jennie later told me that when I began to preach, she felt that I was sharing her story. Everything I said that morning was for her. When I made the altar invitation, she couldn't wait to run to the front. From that day she never looked back. Jesus revolutionized Jennie's life.

If you were to meet her today, you would never know how angry and bitter she had been. She is one of the most compassionate people I know. Jeannie cared for her two children, got married, and became a leader in our worldwide mission effort. She is paying forward the love her Christian friend poured into her. She is pointing people to the Lamb of God, the Savior who rescued her from darkness.

We have the honor of being best men (and maids of honor) at the greatest wedding the world has ever known. We point people to the beautiful and perfect groom . . . to the one who gave all to those He loves . . . to Jesus, the ultimate one who stood in the gap for us all.

THINK ABOUT IT . . .

1. Would you have been attracted or repulsed by John the Baptist? Explain your answer.

2. If John came to your house and had coffee with you, what do you think he might say to you? How would you respond?

3. How did God prepare John (and his parents) for his pivotal role of announcing the Messiah?

4. How would you define and describe true repentance? What are some common excuses people use to avoid genuine change?

5. What are some negative voices in your world? What are some negative messages that come out of your mouth? Look below the surface. What fears and hurts drive those messages?

6. Why is it often easier to tell people about church than to tell them about Jesus?

7. Does the account of John's doubts bother you or encourage you? Explain your response.

8. What is God saying to you through the story of John the Baptist?

7 GIDEON

. . . was sensitive to the voice of God

"The angel of the LORD came and sat down under the oak in Ophrah that belonged to Joash the Abiezrite, where his son Gideon was threshing wheat in a winepress to keep it from the Midianites. When the angel of the LORD appeared to Gideon, he said, 'The LORD is with you, mighty warrior'" (Jud. 6:11–12).

In His incredible grace, wisdom, and power, God sometimes makes cowards into heroes. That's what happened to one person in the Bible you would least expect to stand in the gap during a time of crisis. His name was Gideon.

After God's people conquered the Promised Land and Joshua died, God sent a series of leaders, called judges. Throughout this period, we see a clear historical cycle: God's people fall away from Him; their enemies oppress them; they cry out to God for deliverance; God sends a judge to deliver them; the land is at peace until the judge dies . . . and the cycle begins again.

After forty years of peace, the cycle began again during the life of Gideon. The people "did evil in the eyes of the LORD"

(Jud. 6:1), and this time the Midianites were the enemy that oppressed. In fact, the Israelites were so scared that they abandoned their towns and lived in caves in the mountains. Theirs was an agrarian society; they lived by farming and raising livestock. But when they tried to grow crops and tend sheep and cattle, the Midianites were like a "swarm of locusts" (Jud. 6:5) that destroyed the crops and killed all the livestock. God's people had been conquerors, but now they lived in fear and poverty. Finally, they cried out to the Lord to rescue them.

Into this spiritual darkness, fear, and financial hardship, God sent a prophet to speak words of correction:

> "This is what the LORD, the God of Israel, says: I brought you up out of Egypt, out of the land of slavery. I rescued you from the hand of the Egyptians. And I delivered you from the hand of all your oppressors; I drove them out before you and gave you their land. I said to you, 'I am the LORD your God; do not worship the gods of the Amorites, in whose land you live.' But you have not listened to me" (Jud. 6:8–10).

Grace always includes bad news as well as good news. The bad news is that we're sinners who deserve God's righteous judgment and condemnation. When our hearts are broken because we realize our sin has broken God's heart, we're ready for the good news of forgiveness and restoration. The prophetic message set the stage for God's miracle of deliverance—and as always, it came in a very strange package!

A RELUCTANT LEADER

Gideon was threshing wheat for his family. People usually thresh grain in an open area so the breeze can blow the chaff away from the grain. Yet when the angel of the Lord found Gideon, he was threshing wheat in the confined space of a winepress. Why? He was hiding his wheat (and himself) from the vicious Midianites.

I get the picture of a guy looking over his shoulder to see if anyone is coming. He threw grain up into the air and watched it all fall to the ground in front of him because there was no breeze in the cramped winepress. This guy was scared out of his mind. Suddenly, a mighty angel appeared and announced, "The LORD is with you, mighty warrior" (Jud. 6:12).

Gideon probably thought, *Uh, I think you've got the wrong guy! You see, I'm really not a mighty warrior, and I have no intention of becoming one. You may not know it, but things are pretty tough around here with the Midianites!* Gideon wanted some answers:

> "Pardon me, my lord," Gideon replied, "but if the LORD is with us, why has all this happened to us? Where are all his wonders that our ancestors told us about when they said, 'Did not the LORD bring us up out of Egypt?' But now the LORD has abandoned us and given us into the hand of Midian" (Jud. 6:13).

The Lord didn't bother to enter Gideon's debate about the past, and He didn't answer the accusation of abandonment. He simply gave him clear instructions: "Go in the strength you have and save Israel out of Midian's hand. Am I not sending you?" (Jud. 6:14)

For Gideon, God's answer didn't make sense. Those God had used in the past were great leaders like Abraham, Isaac, Jacob, Moses, and Joshua. Gideon had just been caught hiding in a winepress! He responded, "Pardon me, my lord, but how can I save Israel? My clan is the weakest in Manasseh, and I am the least in my family" (Jud. 6:15).

If you want to be a man or a woman who stands in the gap, you must control what you say to yourself. We're often our own greatest enemy.

Gideon was sure he was making a valid case for God to find someone else. Manasseh was a half-tribe of Joseph. Strike one. His clan was the weakest in the bunch. Strike two. And in his family, Gideon was at the bottom of the list. Strike three.

But God didn't buy Gideon's argument. He told him, "I will be with you, and you will strike down all the Midianites, leaving none alive" (Jud. 6:16).

Sometimes you just have to ignore what people say. If you want to be a man or a woman who stands in the gap, you must control what you say to yourself. We're often our own greatest enemy. With our mouths we can sabotage the calling of God.

I can relate to Gideon's questions and hesitations. When I was growing up, my teachers didn't see me as a star student. In fact, I failed the third grade and had to repeat it because I had a reading problem. My father had left us, and my mother often worked two jobs to make ends meet. To help her, I started working at a grocery store after school when I was about eleven years old. I was just a kid. I had no sense that my life mattered. I certainly didn't grasp God's greater plan for my life. Others may have had grand plans, but not me.

We lived in a tough part of the city. Crime, gangs, drugs, and poverty made us feel like we didn't matter. Every day, survival was my goal. I only hoped to make it through the day. Like Gideon, I was afraid of the known and the unknown. I didn't see Midianites in our neighborhood, but I saw gang members and policemen every day. They were in a constant struggle for power. But the unknown bothered me even more than what I could see. We moved so often that I didn't know where I would sleep each night. We often stayed with my uncles and aunts for periods of time when my mother couldn't afford the rent for an apartment. Day after day, I didn't know if she would have enough money to pay for food, and I didn't know if we would be safe. I lived with a pervasive sense of fear. If there had been a winepress in Humboldt Park, I would have been hiding in it!

Gideon's fear was combined with shame. For generations, God had worked powerfully in the lives of his ancestors, but

Gideon felt abandoned and vulnerable to attacks from his enemies. He felt helpless and hopeless. He saw himself as "the least" of his family. I felt the same way. My mother put much of her attention on my older brothers because they were often in trouble. On many occasions, my mother had to visit their school to meet with the principal and teachers . . . and then there was the police station, and even the hospital. My brother was a gang leader. Once he was stabbed, and he was almost always in trouble. My mother constantly worried about him. I didn't want to cause my mother to worry, so I was a quiet kid. There were many of us at home, but I felt completely alone. Poverty was a daily condition for us. I often went to the store to buy milk, but I waited until no one was in line because I didn't want anyone to know I was using food stamps. I felt ashamed that our family was so poor.

Gideon and I both had concluded that life would never change. We would always be insecure and without purpose. The Midianites were numerous, strong, and violent. In our neighborhood, gangs, violence, and poverty created the same kind of shame and uncertainty.

Gangs and poverty aren't the only threats. Some people are wealthy, but their lives are just as empty as Gideon's. Those in the middle and upper classes feel the pressure of an unknown future and the heartbreak of broken dreams. They may not wonder where they'll sleep or what they'll eat, but they wonder if their lives matter at all. When they look around, they see others—siblings, friends, and neighbors—who seem more successful, popular, and happier. Actually, someone *is* always richer, or better looking, or more popular. Comparison poisons our hearts, so we feel like "the least" in spite of all the things God has done for us.

Gideon saw himself as a punk, but the angel of the Lord had a different opinion of him. The angel made a declaration of Gideon's *future,* not his past; his *potential,* not his limitations. The one hiding in the winepress could become a mighty warrior.

The angel didn't tell Gideon to go in his own wisdom and power. He told him, "Go in the strength you have." What did he have? He was standing in front of God's mighty angel. He had the unlimited resources of Almighty God! If Gideon had focused on his past or his present at that moment, he would have missed an opportunity of a lifetime. But he realized the angel of the Lord represented all the might of heaven. God was giving Gideon a new perspective—of himself, his situation, and the possibilities for deliverance. God was calling him to a higher purpose than mere survival. He was calling him to play a part in rescuing His people and turning their lives around.

When God calls us to stand in the gap, it's not just to help us make it through the day. It's to rescue someone God loves.

When God calls us to stand in the gap, it's not just to help us make it through the day. It's to rescue someone God loves. We don't stand in the gap for ourselves, but for others. We don't act in our own strength. We take bold steps because we trust in God's wisdom and power to accomplish the work that has to be done. Those steps always involve risk. We stand in the gap for a son or daughter, a spouse or parent, a neighborhood or a nation. God's call to stand up for His cause addresses a real need and a desperate situation, and many times we just don't feel up to the challenge.

Though the angel was crystal clear, Gideon wasn't convinced. To him the message from God didn't make sense. Gideon needed more proof.

SO, CONVINCE ME

In response to the angel, Gideon said, "If now I have found favor in your eyes, give me a sign that it is really you talking to me" (Jud. 6:17). Some people assume that Gideon's request for a sign was an indication of sinful unbelief. I don't believe that's the case. God isn't a vending machine. We don't take or leave what He offers. He is a loving Father, King, and Savior. He knows our weaknesses and our doubts. He's well aware that we, like our own children, often need a little help to understand what He tells us.

I often ask God for signs. Sometimes I sense God's direction, but I'm not sure if I'm right about what I think He's telling me. I want Him to make His will clear, so I ask Him for clarification.

When I have important meetings with politicians, I ask God to show me what He wants me to say and do. When we bought the farm to heal and disciple women who had lost hope, I asked God to give us cash to pay for it as a sign the idea was from Him. Without all the money in cash, I wasn't going forward. God provided exactly what we needed.

When Jesus came down the mountain from the experience of transfiguration, He found some of His disciples struggling to help a boy who was possessed by a demon. The boy's father was upset. He had come to them in desperate need, but they had failed to cast the demon out of his son. Jesus asked the man about the boy's history and condition. The dad explained,

> "It has often thrown him into fire or water to kill him. But if you can do anything, take pity on us and help us."
>
> "'If you can'?" said Jesus. "Everything is possible for one who believes."
>
> Immediately the boy's father exclaimed, "I do believe; help me overcome my unbelief!" (Mark 9:22–24)

Jesus didn't walk away from the man because he lacked faith. He didn't make fun of him or rebuke him. Jesus simply answered his request for help in the most convincing way possible: by casting the demon out of his son.

This scene is similar to Gideon's conversation with the angel of the Lord. Gideon was saying, "Lord, I believe, but I need some signs to help me with my unbelief." And the Lord gave him a series of three signs.

In the first one, Gideon brought an offering of meat and bread and placed them on a rock. The angel of the Lord tapped his staff on the offering, and fire consumed the food. The angel of the Lord was answering Gideon's first question: "Why has God let Israel be attacked? Where has he been?" In the first sign, God said, "I'm here!"

Gideon didn't ask for a second sign, but God gave him one. Gideon's father was worshiping Baal instead of the one true God, and he had raised an Asherah pole, a symbol of fertility, next to the altar to Baal. The Lord told Gideon to build a new altar to God, cut down the pole, and use the wood for a fire to sacrifice a bull.

Gideon may have been amazed at the first sign, but this one carried genuine risks. The first one was in private; this one would be a message to his father, his family, and the community of people who worshipped Baal. Gideon was afraid, so he waited until dark to cut down the pole, build the altar, and sacrifice the bull.

Gideon's fear was an appropriate instinct! The men of the town were furious and wanted Gideon's blood. They were ready to execute him on the spot! Surprisingly, Gideon found an unlikely ally: his father. His dad told the angry neighbors that Baal should be able to defend himself.

Gideon may have wondered why a sign from God carried the threat of death with it, but that wasn't the point. The first sign with the fire on the rock was designed to address Gideon's doubts, and with the second sign God established Gideon's reputation as a brave leader. He had been hiding for so long that he needed to do something drastic, something that would get people's attention right away. Later, when he called people to follow him, they needed to know he was a man worthy of their loyalty. Gideon's willingness to stand up to a false god in defiance of his father and his friends was enough to convince them. Now he was ready to lead, and they were ready to follow.

Gideon was finally convinced God had called him to rescue His people from the Midianites. At that point, several armies united in a valley to attack Israel. This time, instead of running and hiding, Gideon became God's warrior: "Then the Spirit of the Lord came on Gideon, and he blew a trumpet, summoning the Abiezrites to follow him. He sent messengers throughout Manasseh, calling them to arms, and also into Asher, Zebulun and Naphtali, so that they too went up to meet them" (Jud. 6:34–35).

As the troops gathered for battle, Gideon asked God for a third sign. We may laugh that he asked God for assurance again and again, but I believe it actually demonstrates Gideon's faithfulness. He wanted to make sure he wasn't imagining the signs or making them up on his own. He needed to know it was God at work. Are we any different?

This time Gideon asked God for a two-part sign: to make a fleece dry when the ground around it was wet one morning, and the next morning to make the fleece wet when there was no dew (Jud. 6:36–40). God gave Gideon the signs he requested. Now he was ready to lead his army in battle. Or was he?

NOT SO FAST!

Gideon had assembled an army of 32,000 farmers and shepherds to fight against the combined forces of the most powerful armies in that part of the world. It was a big challenge, but he was prepared to lead them into battle. Just before the battle opened, God spoke to him and blew his mind: "You have too many men. I cannot deliver Midian into their hands, or Israel would boast against me, 'My own strength has saved me.' Now announce to the army, 'Anyone who trembles with fear may turn back and leave Mount Gilead'" (Jud. 7:2–3).

Too many men! The other army had vastly superior forces, and God told Gideon to announce that any who were afraid could leave! Immediately, 22,000 men bailed out and headed for home. In an instant, Gideon lost more than two-thirds of his army.

But God wasn't finished. He next told Gideon to have his men go to the river for a drink. Those who knelt down to drink were sent home, but those who "lap like dogs" were to remain in Gideon's army. I can imagine Gideon's shock as he watched. Only 300 men lapped water. His army had dwindled from 32,000 to 300!

The Lord let him know this wasn't a mistake: "With the three hundred men that lapped I will save you and give the Midianites into your hands. Let all the others go home" (Jud. 7:7). Gideon had tested God by asking for signs, and then God tested Gideon by reducing his force. As always, God's test stripped him of self-reliance so that he had only one resource: God.

God tested Gideon by reducing his force. As always, God's test stripped him of self-reliance so that he had only one resource: God.

STRANGE ORDERS

The opposing armies of perhaps 135,000 soldiers had swords, spears, and armor. God told Gideon to arm his little band of men with trumpets and candles. God's instructions for the army seemed most unusual, but they were clear. By this time, the men really must have trusted Gideon, because these were probably the strangest orders ever given to an army.

In another act of grace and patience, God told Gideon that if he was afraid of the upcoming battle, he and his servant could sneak up on the enemy camp and listen to the sentries. What they heard would give them courage.

Gideon wasn't one to miss out on additional confirmation, so he and his servant went down to the enemy camp at night, listened, and overheard a sentry tell his friend about a dream of a huge loaf of bread crushing the Midianite camp. The second soldier responded, "This can be nothing other than the sword of Gideon son of Joash, the Israelite. God has given the Midianites and the whole camp into his hands" (Jud. 7:14).

That did it! Gideon didn't just accept the overheard dream as an interesting coincidence; he realized it was another sign from a patient and mighty God. At the moment of the greatest challenge of Gideon's life, God came through again with His presence, power, and purpose. Gideon needed to prepare his men for the coming battle, but he stopped to worship the Lord before he took another step.

When he got back to his camp, he announced that God was going to give them a great victory. (I'm not sure he told them about the loaf of bread.) He divided his forces into three companies, and he gave each man a trumpet and an empty jar with a lit candle inside.

> "Watch me," he told them. "Follow my lead. When I get to the edge of the camp, do exactly as I do. When I and all who are with me blow our trumpets, then from all around the camp blow yours and shout, 'For the LORD and for Gideon'" (Jud. 7:17–18).

Gideon led his men through the darkness to the enemy camp. In armies of that day, a soldier blowing a trumpet typically signaled a force of about 1,000 men, much the way trumpeters were used by armies during the American Civil War. When Gideon's 300 men suddenly blew their trumpets and broke the jars to let their lights shine, the enemy armies thought 300,000 men surrounded them! In their fear and confusion, the Midianites and their allies attacked each other. The survivors fled for their lives. When the victory was assured, Gideon sent word to the rest of Israel to join the pursuit. In the end, it was one of the greatest—and most unlikely—military victories the world has ever known, led by one of the most unlikely warriors in history.

In the end, God received glory for the victory. Gideon couldn't claim credit; he had taken plenty of time to be convinced God was in the plan. The soldiers couldn't claim credit because the method of warfare was too "out of the box." It had to be God. When the angel of the Lord first appeared in the winepress, Gideon listened. And he kept listening as the Lord slowly convinced him that He was real and His instructions were trustworthy. We might think that Gideon was wrong to ask God for signs, but I believe the opposite is true: Gideon was sensitive to God and responsive to His voice to stand in the gap for his people against a fierce enemy. God challenged Gideon to trust Him, and God was pleased with his faith and courage.

A LISTENING EAR

Gideon's response to God teaches us many important lessons for today. From his story, we learn the importance of: (1) discovering God's perspective of our identity; (2) engaging God with questions and asking for signs; (3) realizing that God often removes things from our lives so we will trust Him more fully; and (4) understanding that crazy instructions may just be His plan for us.

The power of self-talk

One's sense of identity can be terribly limiting or wonderfully inspiring. Gideon had perceived himself as a loser, "the least" in his clan and his family. Our self-talk—especially after we have experienced failure or rejection—speaks volumes about what we really believe about God and ourselves. If we call ourselves horrible names, it's a sign that we've internalized the negative experience. We didn't just fail; *we're failures*. We didn't just suffer rejection; *we're rejects*. The painful experience has become our identity. Failure, though, doesn't have to define a person.

One's sense of identity can be terribly limiting or wonderfully inspiring.

Many people around us (even at church) have concluded, "God may be out there somewhere, but He really doesn't care about me." Whether they are rich or poor, this conclusion makes them feel like victims. They believe God (or life) has let them down. They had high hopes, but all they have seen is failure. As a matter of fact, they enjoy feeling sorry for themselves. They wallow in self-pity, resenting those who have hurt them as well as those who have risen above their circumstances to make something of their lives. They say to themselves:

"Everyone is against me."

"I never do anything right."

"I have no future."

"Whatever I try blows up in my face."

"It'll never get any better than this."

"There's no use. I might as well give up."

"No wonder my father left me."

"God must be against me."

Comparison is the fuel of a victim mentality. When people look around and complain that someone else has a better spouse, nicer kids, a more fulfilling job, a newer car, or a bigger house, they feel like losers. Do you want to know what I think? Who cares what other people have? That type of thinking produces nothing good. As a matter of fact, this negative view is a brother to greed because it's never satisfied, and it's a cousin to envy because it never celebrates another person's success. We should be happy when someone else gets a raise or a nice car, and we should celebrate people when they're promoted or win awards. We shouldn't waste time and energy complaining and comparing.

People who perceive themselves as victims are usually self-absorbed. They can only think about their own pain, their own comfort, and their own desires. They don't see themselves as leaders. Instead, they demand attention. They are miserable, and their negativity makes others miserable. They are slaves, chained to their past wounds and failures. If they persist in this kind of talking, they reach a point where they can't imagine ever being free from those chains.

The way we think about ourselves shapes our words and our actions. Gideon hid in the winepress because he thought of himself as a loser and his circumstances as hopeless. When he began to see himself from God's point of view, his words and actions changed. When we begin to see ourselves from God's perspective, we too will change. Then we will get to be a part of the greatest movement this world has ever known—seeing lost people experience the love of God and watching His kingdom grow here on earth.

Having our identity in Christ isn't a one-time event that lasts for all time. Negative messages from our families, our culture, and our own minds will keep coming at us, so we need to continually reinforce our new identity with truths from God's Word, talks with Christian friends, and clear sermons that tell us who we really are. It's a battle, and it's one we will lose if we don't get it right. The Bible repeatedly tells us to think, consider, and remember the grace of God. We need those reminders because it's so easy to forget! We need to find people who are a step or two ahead of us on the road of living according to our new identity. Call them, hang out with them, ask questions, listen, and follow their example of tenacious faith—especially when you feel like giving up.

Sometimes living as a victim feels so right that people refuse to give it up even after they discover the freedom and power of God. They become comfortable with their negativity, maybe because it's all they've ever known, or maybe it's the only way they know to get attention. Whatever the reason, their negative perception is a prison. God sometimes brings them to a point of brokenness to let them see how much they need Him. If they're willing, He will change them, fill them, restore them, and give them something to live for. Victims then become overcomers. I've seen dramatic transformations many times in the lives of helpless, hopeless men and women. I've witnessed the amazing change that happens when grace melts a person's heart and gives them a purpose far bigger than themselves. It's beautiful.

Never forget: failure is not the defining identity of a person; it's only an event.

Engaging God

As we become more attuned to the voice of God, we realize God has no problem with our questions and our desire for signs, but we don't need to be ridiculous about it. We don't need a sign to know we need to get up in the morning or read our Bibles or serve God. But when we sense God is telling us to do something beyond our normal capacity—like Gideon becoming a mighty warrior—it's entirely proper to ask Him for confirming signs. In all meaningful relationships, we expect an honest exchange, and we value the process of communication and understanding. Should it be any different in our relationship with God? I don't think so. God wasn't upset with Job for asking, time and time again, why he experienced such pain and loss.

When we sense God is telling us to do something beyond our normal capacity—like Gideon becoming a mighty warrior—it's entirely proper to ask Him for confirming signs.

When Lot was living in Sodom, God told Abraham that He was going to destroy the city. Abraham asked God if He would spare the city if there were fifty righteous people there. God agreed. Abraham kept lowering the number in increments down to ten, and God agreed each time. This exchange tells me that God is incredibly gracious with those who are willing to engage with Him—people like you and me. God invites us to reason with Him and to interact with Him like a child talks to a wise and loving parent.

Let's be honest: sometimes we ask questions again and again—of a spouse, a parent, a friend, or God—when we really don't want a response. Our underlying motives make a difference. The opening chapters of Luke record that when the angel Gabriel visited Zechariah and Mary (on separate occasions), they asked similar questions: "How can this happen?" But we see that God rebuked Zechariah for unbelief while He rewarded Mary for her faith. Be honest, then, about the motive underneath your questions.

Feeling vulnerable

Many people believe that when God calls them to do something, resources will suddenly appear. That may happen, but Gideon experienced just the opposite. God stripped away Gideon's resources until Gideon and his army were completely dependent on Him. We see this principle frequently in the Bible. Joseph had two dreams that he would save his family, but he suffered betrayal, slavery, and many years in prison before his time came. Saul offered David his armor for the fight with Goliath, but David took only his sling and five stones. Jesus preached to thousands and performed miracles, but only 120 faithful people were in the upper room when the Spirit came at Pentecost. The great apostle Paul had vision, wisdom, and zeal, but God gave him a "thorn in the flesh" to make him more humble and dependent.

When God calls you to do something for Him, don't be surprised when resources you have counted on disappear. You might even experience new stresses in your finances, your health, or your career. That doesn't mean you're in sin or that God has abandoned you. It probably means that God wants to do something more wonderful than you could possibly imagine. If you complain and walk away, you'll miss the miracle. But if you trust God when assets are depleted, you might just see God work in a way that brings Him the most glory.

It's important to realize that God didn't take away Gideon's resources until He had confirmed his calling. It was only after Gideon was convinced by the signs and called his army to join him that God shrunk the army down from 32,000 to 300. By the time that happened, Gideon was already "all in." He didn't doubt God when the instructions didn't seem to make sense.

Gideon was challenged when God sent most of the soldiers home before the battle, but the real lesson was for God's people. When the little squad of 300 men defeated the combined armies united against Israel, everybody knew that Almighty God had delivered them. There was no confusion about who deserved the glory. Can you imagine the conversations around the dinner table and at the market when those 300 men went home and told their story? People were amazed—not at Gideon's leadership, but at Gideon's amazing God.

In the same way, when our resources are stripped away, God hasn't abandoned us. He's giving us the opportunity to watch Him do incredible things in our families, our workplaces, our churches, and our communities—and when He does them, He will get all the glory.

> People were amazed—not at Gideon's leadership, but at Gideon's amazing God.

"Insane" instructions

God often works through normal routines, but occasionally He breaks the mold. God's divine instructions may require doing something completely out of the ordinary. Just because they may seem a bit crazy doesn't mean they are a result of eating a deep-dish pizza too late at night.

We often make the mistake of putting God into a box of American culture, assuming that He will resolve everything quickly. (As I like to say, this isn't Burger King, so you can't always "Have it your way!") God doesn't fit into *any* box! God's plans are sometimes totally different from what you may have in mind.

Our assignments are connected to a set of instructions. When Joshua led the people of God out of the desert and into the Promised Land, they were ready for battle. One of their first stops was the fortified city of Jericho. Instead of issuing orders for a line of attack, God told them to march around the city for seven days, and seven times on the seventh day. After marching in the desert for forty years, that plan had to have sounded ridiculous! But they obeyed God's crazy instructions, and when they blew the trumpets on the seventh day, the walls miraculously fell (Josh. 6).

When about 20,000 people (5,000 men and their families) followed Jesus but had nothing to eat, the disciples knew they didn't have enough money to buy sufficient food at the local grocery store. Jesus told them to have the people sit down in groups of fifty. Then, with only a boy's sack lunch, He fed them all . . . and had twelve baskets of leftovers! (Matt. 14:13–21; John 6:1–13) What do you think the disciples were thinking when Jesus took the boy's lunch and thanked God for dinner? Had they realized by that time that limited resources didn't limit Jesus? Have we realized that fact?

Our assignment is connected to a set of instructions. But the resulting miracle is connected to a set of instructions, too! People complain, "The grass is greener on the other side." The fact is, the grass is greener where it's watered and fertilized. God gives us directions—sometimes ones that make no sense to us—and it's up to us to follow them.

TUNING OUR EARS

The best part of Gideon's story is that no one is beyond the voice, the love, and the purposes of God. Gideon was an outcast, even in his own family. As he hid in the winepress, he seemed to have no talents, no resources, and no remarkable character traits. He hadn't heard God's voice before. The only voices he had heard were from his unbelieving father and his fearful culture. But when God spoke, Gideon made a choice to listen and respond. I admire him because he just put himself out there. Now that's faith.

When we ask God for signs, it's between Him and us. We may ask a family member or a friend for advice and feedback, but that's not the kind of sign I'm talking about. In our own hearts, we need to be still enough to hear God.

Years ago, some church leaders came to me and asked if our church would host a citywide youth conference. We were swamped with projects at the time, so I told them we couldn't do it. A few weeks later I went to a men's conference where I had been asked to speak. That night there was only one other speaker. I got to the auditorium early and sat in the back. As I sat there, I heard a voice in my ear that said, "Choco, you should do the youth conference." I went through all the reasons to decline, but the voice was persistent. After a while, I prayed, "Father, if You want our church to host this event, tell the other guy speaking tonight to give me a word from You." I didn't know the man, so I felt safe that this was a sign that would never happen.

I was the second speaker, so I sat quietly in the back as the first man spoke. In the middle of his talk, he stopped and turned to the director of the event. He asked, "Who is the man sitting in the back?"

The director said, "That's Pastor Choco from New Life in Chicago. He's giving the message after yours."

The speaker looked at me and said, "Pastor Choco, stand up. I have a word for you."

I wanted to run and hide, but I stood up as every head turned to see me. He then said, "God wants you to go and do what He has called you to do." That was all he said to me. I sat down, and he then immediately returned to his message.

Well, I couldn't argue with God about this. My excuses and reasons were over. I had asked for a sign, and God gave it. But that's not the end of the story.

To prepare for the event, I invited one hundred youth pastors from around the city to come to our church for planning and prayer. I bought enough sandwiches and drinks for all of them. Just before noon, we were ready for them to come. None came. Not a single one. I wasn't upset. I didn't question God's call to have the event at our church because it had already been made crystal clear to me. I just picked up a sandwich (I had my choice) and had lunch by myself.

The next week, I scheduled another meeting. A few came. We planned another and another until we had enough involvement to make a difference. At the conference, thousands of young people came and were blessed. God's voice had been unmistakable the entire time, but He had stripped away the normal resources so I would trust Him more than ever.

The ability to be sensitive to the voice of God isn't reserved for the super Christian. God desperately wants to connect with each of us in a real relationship. In Jesus' great prayer, He said, "Now this is eternal life: that they may know you, the only true God, and Jesus Christ, whom you have sent" (John 17:3). Paul said, "I consider everything a loss because of the surpassing worth of knowing Christ Jesus my Lord, for whose sake I have lost all things. I consider them garbage, that I may gain Christ. . . . I want to know Christ—yes, to know the power of his resurrection and participation in his sufferings" (Phil. 3:8, 10).

The ability to be sensitive to the voice of God isn't reserved for the super Christian. God desperately wants to connect with each of us in a real relationship.

I have never heard the audible voice of God, but I have heard Him speak. About six years into our marriage, Elizabeth and I weren't doing too well. We were struggling, and all I could think of was that it was time for a divorce. That was an easy way for me to think because that's all I had ever known. Except for two of my aunts, every marriage on my mother's side ended in divorce. You might think that's not too bad, but my mother was one of nineteen brothers and sisters!

Everything changed for me the day I went to a Promise Keepers Conference with a group of men from our church. I thought we would just take a trip, get away, and hang out. How cool is that? But God had something much more interesting planned for me. The stadium was huge—70,000 men in one place—worshiping, crying, hearing from God. I had never seen anything like it, ever. I was so excited!

I don't know how it happened, but I found myself all the way in the front. I was sitting right beside the big stage. I heard a terrific speaker, but I don't remember his name. I'm sure he was a popular Christian leader, but I didn't hear anyone but God that day. He said to me, "Do you love your brother?" Then He repeated, "Do you love your African-American brother? Do you love your Hispanic brother?"

I answered, "Yeah, I do!"

Then He said, "But have you told him?"

I suddenly realized that I never tell people I love them. I began to cry, and I couldn't stop crying. I sat on the floor right in front of the stage asking God for forgiveness. I realized I didn't know how to love, and I needed His help. The place was filled with the power and presence of God. The speaker then asked us to go around and encourage each other. Everyone was hugging and crying.

As I was hugging some guy, I felt the still voice of God, "Elizabeth is your wife. Love her."

At that moment, I realized I hadn't loved her the way Jesus loved me. He died for me. And what was I willing to do for her—divorce her at the first sign of trouble? My heart broke. All I wanted to do was get back home. Elizabeth will tell you that early in our marriage I wasn't much for talking. Thankfully, I've changed, but back then I was a block of ice. I went home and immediately told Elizabeth, "We need to talk."

She looked at me and said in her quiet way, "Okay."

I talked and talked and talked. I asked her to forgive me. I shared my experience at the conference, and I told her I felt God's presence like never before. She listened. It took a while for all the accumulated hurt and misunderstandings to be resolved, but this day was the start.

I'll never forget how God spoke to me—so strong, with so much love. I can't wrap my head around the love of God! I didn't deserve a second chance. And our marriage didn't deserve a second chance, but He gave it to us anyway. I felt compelled to love my wife. I had to because the love of God had become so real to me! I felt compelled to love my brothers and sisters. I no longer had a choice.

Paul explained how the love of God becomes so strong that it pours out of us:

> "For Christ's love compels us, because we are convinced that one died for all, and therefore all died. And he died for all, that those who live should no longer live for themselves but for him who died for them and was raised again" (2 Cor. 5:14–15).

Sometimes, the best way to stand in the gap is to love . . . *really* love. Not "I can't live without you" one day and "I'm out of here!" the next. So many men and women need the faith and courage of Gideon for their marriages and their families. Gideon needed to be strong for others, because others were depending on his leadership, integrity, and faithfulness. They were looking for someone to lead them, to give them direction, but Gideon first needed to know that God was for him. Once he knew God was with him, there was no stopping him. He threw himself out there, trusted God, and changed lives.

I wonder what would have happened if I had walked away from our marriage when times were tough. Where would I be, and where would Elizabeth and the children be today? Last June Elizabeth and I celebrated twenty-five years of marriage. The lessons I learned long ago when God spoke to me at that men's conference have been a constant source of hope and direction. I honestly don't know what I would do without my wife—and she can't live without me either. (I think I heard her say that once). I heard God's voice that day. I listened and responded. It wasn't easy, but God restored something precious that had been broken.

If you attune your ears to hear God's voice, you can be sure He will give you words of correction and encouragement. He will give you instructions so that you tap into His power and love to overcome difficult circumstances. He will assure you of

His presence and power, and you will experience a deep sense of His peace. He will amaze you, and He will bless you. A loving Father always blesses the obedience of His children.

Don't let the wounds and fears of the past dictate your present and your future. Hear God's voice. Be strong and brave.

He is still speaking. Are you listening, mighty warrior?

THINK ABOUT IT . . .

1. How are the culture and conditions of Gideon's Israel similar to ours today, and how are they different?

2. What kind of self-talk do people engage in when they feel like "the least" in their family and community? What names do they call themselves? Where do those messages originate?

3. How would you define and describe a *victim mentality*? Why does it seem so attractive and powerful to some people? How can it be broken?

4. Before you read this chapter, did you think it was right or wrong for people to ask God for signs? How about now?

5. Why is it important to engage God and ask Him questions the way a loved child talks to a parent? Is this how you relate to God? Why or why not?

6. How do you respond when you don't have enough resources? Do you feel anxious, or do you believe it's an opportunity to see God do something extraordinary? Explain your answer.

7. How can you become more sensitive to the voice of God?

8. What is God saying to you through the story of Gideon?

8 DEBORAH

. . . earned a reputation of wisdom and strength

"Deborah, a prophet, the wife of Lappidoth, was leading Israel at that time. She held court under the Palm of Deborah between Ramah and Bethel in the hill country of Ephraim, and the Israelites went up to her to have their disputes decided. She sent for Barak son of Abinoam from Kedesh in Naphtali and said to him, 'The LORD, the God of Israel, commands you: "Go, take with you ten thousand men of Naphtali and Zebulun and lead them up to Mount Tabor"'" (Jud. 4:4–6).

Gideon was one of several leaders God called to deliver His people during the era of the judges. As we saw in the previous chapter, his victory over the Midianites was clear evidence of God's power and forgiveness. But after another period of Israel's disobedience during that era, God's people again found themselves in trouble because of their sin. God gave them into the hands of Jabin, king of Canaan, and his ruthless army commander, Sisera. For twenty years, Jabin and his men "cruelly oppressed" God's people. Theirs was the most formidable force in the region, with 900 iron chariots supporting the infantry.

GOD SENT A WOMAN

This time when the people cried out to the Lord for deliverance, God sent a woman. Deborah led Israel as a prophet and a judge, unique roles for a woman in that time and culture. She was the only female judge during the period between the conquest of the Promised Land under Joshua and the establishment of the kingdom under Saul, David, and Solomon. Although individuals, families, and the entire culture had been weakened by corruption and defiled by idolatry, Deborah provided strong leadership.

She must have been a remarkable woman. She first earned the respect of God's people by her wisdom and maturity as all of Israel came to air their disputes and hear her judgments. She combined the traits of compassion, justice, and strength. People trusted her to solve their problems because they knew she depended on God for her insight, and she cared about them. When the nation needed a leader to stand up to the Canaanite oppressors, Deborah was a symbol of strength and stability.

When the nation needed a leader to stand up to the Canaanite oppressors, Deborah was a symbol of strength and stability.

Although the story of Deborah is fairly short, we can learn a lot by noticing details in the biblical account. Names mentioned in the Bible are often significant. Deborah's name means *bee.* A bee is industrious and ranks as one of the most intelligent creatures in the animal kingdom. Bees are known to have a sophisticated form of communication and an incredible guidance system. And they have stingers—they may be small, but they pack a punch!

The names of locations found in Deborah's story are also indicators of her God-given assignment. She held court under a palm tree—a symbol of Deborah's standing with God, or perhaps, that righteous judgments were given from that place. As the psalmist noted, "The righteous will flourish like a palm tree" (Ps. 92:12).

The palm tree was located between Ramah and Bethel in the hill country of Ephraim (Jud. 4:5). Ramah refers to a "high place" used in idol worship; Bethel means "house of God;" and Ephraim means "fruitfulness." Together, these important words suggest that Deborah was called by God to judge Israel from the place or position of righteousness, to stand in the gap and speak against idolatry, and to turn God's children back to the house of God. The result would be an abundance of choice fruit instead of the fruit of destruction. Deborah's job was clear: to declare the Word of God and to direct His people to His presence.

Deborah led her people with clarity and purpose because she understood her role. She is not only known as a judge and a prophet, but also as "a mother in Israel" (Jud. 5:7). In this role, she provided nourishment and comfort during a time of chaos and instability. She was a tower of strength under the palm tree. She provided a place where God's people could find rest, assurance, and spiritual insight.

I envision that palm tree as the hangout spot where everyone gathered to discuss important issues. It was the place to be, where the locals and not-so-locals gathered to find answers to difficult questions. It was a meeting place where Deborah served the people in family matters and where social concerns were voiced. The palm tree is a symbol of justice and peace, plenty and fruitfulness, majesty and military triumph. And although the people may not have felt that they were living in a time of justice or peace, that spot served as a hopeful reminder of God's promise to them. Centuries later, when Jesus was on His way to Jerusalem, the people felt such hope in their hearts that they gathered palm branches and went to meet Him shouting, "Hosanna!" (John 12:12–13)

Deborah's palm tree reminds me of our church's New Life Café. As the pastor, I have a nice office because people spent a lot of thought and effort decorating and furnishing it. Yet I tend to spend much time in the café and have most of my meetings there. The café used to be a liquor store and a popular gang hangout. The corner was what we called *hot*. Drive-by shootings were common. Our church was just down the block, but everyone avoided that corner. As a matter of fact, I never allowed my young children to walk near there—not even in broad daylight. It was just too dangerous.

Years later our church bought the place, cleaned it up, and opened the café. As I sit there and meet with individuals, politicians, hospital administrators, or school officials, I sometimes feel like Deborah under the palm tree administrating God's justice and wisdom. I meet with couples who want to divorce, with children who want to rebel, and with politicians who struggle to serve the community. I disciple young adults and meet with young pastors. I hear their stories, listen to their dreams, and ask God to give me the wisdom to say the right thing. I usually sit near the front and beside the window so I can see people who walk by on the sidewalk. I want them to know that I'm here in their community. I hope my presence provides the same kind of comfort and wisdom Deborah gave her people.

During a very difficult time in the life of God's people, Deborah was fully present. When a critical moment—a national emergency—surfaced, she was ready. Her heart was in tune with the voice of God. She sent for Barak, her army's commander, and told him:

> "The LORD, the God of Israel, commands you: 'Go, take with you ten thousand men of Naphtali and Zebulun and lead them up to Mount Tabor. I will lure Sisera, the commander of Jabin's army, with his chariots and his troops to the Kishon River and give him into your hands'" (Jud. 4:6–7).

Barak's name means "lightning," yet when he heard God's orders, he was hesitant. He told Deborah, "If you go with me, I will go; but if you don't go with me, I won't go" (Jud. 4:8). In other words, "I ain't going out there against a huge army and 900 chariots by myself!"

Deborah responded with calm and confidence. She didn't blow up, and she didn't use the moment to throw her power around. She simply told him, "Okay, that's fine. I'll go with you, but when God works, you won't get the honor for the victory. People will know that the great general Sisera was defeated by a woman." (And she wasn't even talking about herself! See Jud. 4:17–21.)

You may tend to think of Barak as a wimp, but that's the wrong conclusion. He was outgunned, outmanned, and overmatched, leading a poorly equipped, pitiful army of 10,000 against a much larger force with iron chariots (which at that time would have been the equivalent of M1 Abrams Tanks in today's Army). Barak's willingness to lead demonstrated remarkable bravery. Certainly, he showed some doubts, but he was far more courageous than most of us would have been in the same situation. Indeed, he is included among the heroes of great faith and bold action in Hebrews 11 (vv. 32–34).

Instead of demeaning Barak as a coward, I applaud his wisdom in asking Deborah to join him in leading the army. The people trusted her, and her presence would provide confidence that the Lord would give them a remarkable victory. I also suspect that Barak had far more confidence in Deborah's ability to hear God's voice than in his own. Her presence was encouragement for his men and for him.

The soldiers knew Deborah's reputation. They realized God was with her. Seeing her at the head of the army gave them confidence that God was going to do something incredible to rescue their nation. In every organization—families, churches, companies, and nations—people draw courage and strength from noble leaders. Deborah was a woman worth following into battle.

In every organization—families, churches, companies, and nations—people draw courage and strength from noble leaders.

Deborah ordered Barak to attack the superior forces: "Go! This is the day the LORD has given Sisera into your hands. Has not the LORD gone ahead of you?" (Jud. 4:14) As Barak led the charge down Mount Tabor, God sent a torrential rainstorm. The wheels of the enemy chariots mired in the mud, and Barak's army routed Sisera's forces! (Jud. 5:19–21)

The military victory was so sweeping and (from a human perspective) unexpected that there was no doubt whose power was behind it. Deborah and Barak knew the glory belonged to the Lord. They didn't jockey for honor. They didn't try to get their pictures on the front page of the paper. In a beautiful depiction of unity and humility, the two of them led the choir in a song to celebrate the victory.

After Gideon's battle, 300 eyewitnesses had returned to their communities to tell others what great things the Lord had done. But after Deborah and Barak led the army in battle, 10,000 evangelists went home to talk about God's power and glory. Some of them may have ridden home in iron chariots, spoils from the battlefield. When God gives, He gives in abundance.

After the battle, God gave Israel peace for the next forty years.

THE ROLE OF WOMEN

Where did Deborah get her authority to lead? The Bible doesn't give us any explanation other than to say that she "held court under the Palm of Deborah . . . and the Israelites went up to her to have their disputes decided" (Jud. 4:5). At a crucial time, we find Deborah in the place of her assignment and the people coming to her for help.

Various denominations have different interpretations of the Scriptures, but it seems odd in this age of equality that I am so often criticized for my belief that God uses women in leadership roles in the church. Throughout Scripture and church history, women have upheld a great spiritual legacy, yet the church is often where women's gifts are questioned and stifled.

God created the universe with order and hierarchy. When He created Adam, He recognized that "it is not good for the man to be alone" (Gen. 2:18). He created Eve from a rib from Adam's side—not from his head or his foot, but from his side to be a partner and helper.

Genesis says, "God created mankind in his own image . . . male and female he created them" (Gen. 1:27). Both men and women reflect the image of God: tenderness and strength, boldness and caution, compassion and bravery. These characteristics aren't divided in sharp contrasts between men and women, but sociologists, psychologists, and observant people throughout the ages have noticed a difference.

One of the most remarkable facts of the Gospels is that the first people to see the resurrected Christ were "Mary Magdalene and the other Mary" (Matt. 28:1). In the patriarchal Jewish and Roman cultures, women weren't even allowed to give testimony in court. So the fact that women were the first to testify to the resurrection of Christ is strong evidence that the account was not fictional. New Testament scholar N. T. Wright comments on the role of women—and particularly, Mary Magdalene:

> "They would never, ever, ever have invented the idea that it was a woman—a woman with a known background of emotional instability, but the main point is that it was a woman—to whom had been entrusted the earth-shattering message that Jesus was alive again. . . .

> It is Mary: not Peter, not John, not James the brother of the Lord, but Mary, who becomes the apostle to the apostles, the primary Christian witness, the first Christian evangelist. This is so striking, so unexpected, so embarrassing to some early Christians . . . that it cannot be accidental. It cannot be accidental for John and the other writers. And I dare to say it cannot be accidental in the purposes of God."[26]

The purposes of God include honoring a woman as the "apostle to the apostles," which astounded people in the first century. If we understand the significance, it amazes us still today.

In John's gospel, the first person who became an evangelist was the woman Jesus met at the well in Sychar. Her status as a woman was a major limitation in that culture, but this particular woman would have been rejected for additional reasons. Ethnically, she was a Samaritan, people who were despised by the Jews. Morally, she had had five husbands and was living with a man who wasn't her husband. She was an outcast among outcasts. During Jesus' conversation with her, the twelve disciples were more concerned about lunch than her salvation. They couldn't understand why in the world Jesus would go out of His way to talk to a woman—especially *that* woman!

Yet when she experienced the cleansing flood of Jesus' living water, no one had to give her lessons on sharing her faith, and they didn't have to talk to her about her motives. John describes her enthusiasm: "Then, leaving her water jar, the woman went back to the town and said to the people, 'Come, see a man who told me everything I ever did. Could this be the Messiah?' . . . Many of the Samaritans from that town believed in him because of the woman's testimony" (John 4:28–29, 39).

We have other accounts of the importance of women in the biblical narrative. Some of the closest followers of Jesus were women, and they contributed financially to His ministry (Luke 8:1–3). Philip the evangelist had four daughters who prophesied (Acts 21:8–9).

The Holy Spirit, the divine author of the Scriptures, makes sure we see the unusual and prominent role of women throughout the story of redemption. Deborah is only one of many stories, but she is the first of the gifted and godly women thrust into leadership during times of calamity and suffering. God used her to provide wise and trusted leadership in a day when her people were oppressed, and God uses wise and trusted women today to provide leadership in the church. We need their hearts, their courage, and their compassion.

God uses wise and trusted women today to provide leadership in the church. We need their hearts, their courage, and their compassion.

The debate about the role of women in leadership is complex and often emotional, but women are called to leadership in the same way men are called by God. It's remarkable that God chose Deborah, Mary Magdalene, the woman at the well, Priscilla, Philip's daughters and other women for prominent roles in restrictive cultures that normally would have limited their influence. God seemed to have bigger plans for women than their societies realized.

Another factor in determining the role of women is the failure of men to step into the gap and take leadership. When men don't step up, they create a vacuum. Women sense the need and out of hearts of compassion try to meet it. Single mothers take charge every day because husbands and fathers are absent for any number of reasons. Women are simply doing what needs to be done because men have abdicated their roles. This factor explains why some women find themselves in leadership, but even when men play appropriate roles, women have a place at the leadership table.

When Paul wrote to correct wrong thinking about theology and relationships in the Galatian church, he made a startling comment: "In Christ Jesus you are all children of God through faith, for all of you who were baptized into Christ have clothed yourselves with Christ. There is neither Jew nor Greek, neither slave nor free, nor is there male and female, for you are all one in Christ Jesus. If you belong to Christ, then you are Abraham's seed, and heirs according to the promise" (Gal. 3:26–29).

In the first-century world, only male children received an inheritance, and the oldest son received a disproportionate share.

Paul turned that idea upside down when he said, "In Christ Jesus you are all (both men and women in the church) children of God through faith." In other words, women have exactly the same rights and privileges as men in God's plans. Paul reemphasized the point by listing the classic insiders and outsiders in the culture—Jew and Greek, free and slave, male and female—and he made the astounding assertion that all are "one in Christ Jesus."

We may debate the biblical and cultural influences that shape our positions on the role of women, but in the story of Deborah, it is undeniable that God chose her to be the leader of His people during a turbulent time in the nation's history. She stood in the gap because God called her to lead His people with wisdom, justice, and strength.

Let me say a few things to women and to men.

Women:

- Deborah earned her position of leadership by listening to God, trusting Him for wisdom, and faithfully serving the people who came to her. She didn't resort to manipulation. She didn't see others as nuisances, even though, of course, she had to hear a lot of bickering in the disputes. Over years of dedication and love to help people, she earned the admiration of the people of God.

- Deborah stepped up to lead her people when God called her. When a man hesitated, she stepped in again to reassure him and go with him into battle. Follow her example.

Men:

- The story of Deborah shows that women have a God-given calling in His grand plan to redeem the world from sin and death. There's no indication Deborah was His second choice when the Canaanite army threatened her people. As men, we need to honor women and give them room to serve the Lord, His church, and the community.

- Don't leave a leadership vacuum in your family or your church. Don't compete with women to serve God, but don't fade into the wallpaper and fail to shoulder your part of the load. Man up. Get in the game.

- Don't berate Barak for depending on Deborah for support in a time of crisis. Realize he was "lightning," a fierce and noble warrior, a man who was willing to lead God's army in battle against a superior foe. Still, he benefited from the reassurance of a leader who was highly respected for her connection with God—he needed Deborah. They made a

We need to honor women and give them room to serve the Lord, His church, and the community.

great team. Their song of praise in Judges 5 is a beautiful scene of the two of them pointing to God to honor Him.

- Celebrate women who lead with grace and strength. Honor them, compliment them, and support them with all the resources you can find to help them succeed. If you see them as partners in God's grand purposes, you will help each other instead of competing for attention and applause.

INSPIRED BY DEBORAH

My mother is a wonderful example of a woman who stood in the gap for her kids when a man wasn't around. After my father left, she could have collapsed in depression and discouragement, but she stepped up to provide a safe and loving home for my brothers and me. Single mothers live under severe strains and demands. I have the greatest admiration for them as they trust God and impart faith, love, and strength to their kids.

Women, God has called you to be His priests, prophets, and servants. Serve with joy and humility, and try not to let another person's insecurity limit your effectiveness. In all relationships, communicate clearly, avoid demands, and find ways to make things work so everyone fulfills his or her role in God's kingdom. Don't settle for being overlooked, or worse, being ridiculed for wanting to serve the Lord with gladness and strength. You may be frustrated with a man who doesn't appreciate your talents and your calling, but be patient. In God's timing, the door will open for you.

Let your speech be seasoned with salt. Believe in the power of prayer. Be an example in your family and with your friends. Earn the trust of those who know you best, and listen to the input of those in authority. If they are insecure and limit your involvement, excel in the opportunities you have, and trust that God will give you additional opportunities in the future.

God continues to raise up strong, gifted women to lead nations in the spirit of Deborah. Golda Meir led Israel through tumultuous years in the 1970s, including the Yom Kippur War in 1974. Margaret Thatcher was known as "The Iron Lady" for her toughness in uncompromising domestic politics in Great Britain and her stance against tyranny worldwide. And currently Angela Merkel is the strongest voice in the European Union as Chancellor of Germany.

God sometimes uses tragedies to give women their biggest platform to serve Him. Jim and Elisabeth Elliott were committed to take the gospel to "the uttermost parts of the earth." With a few other brave companions, they moved to Ecuador in 1956, hoping to reach the Huaorani, a tribe that had never had contact with the outside world. They knew it was dangerous, so they slowly began to make elaborate overtures to show they were friendly. Their efforts must not have been convincing. One day, shortly after Jim and four other men landed a single engine plane on a remote beach in the jungle, Huaorani warriors stormed out of the bushes and speared the five of them. No one survived.

God sometimes uses tragedies to give women their biggest platform to serve Him.

Elisabeth was suddenly a widow with a ten-month old daughter. Instead of giving up in anger and despair, she determined that her husband's death should not be in vain. After a couple of years of preparation, she and another grieving widow made contact with the tribe and eventually moved to their village. She learned their language, translated the New Testament for them, and led many of them to Christ—including some of the men who had murdered her husband.

Through her suffering and service, Elliott discovered rich spiritual lessons about how to respond to blessings and heartaches. In her book, *Passion and Purity*, she reflected,

> "If we hold tightly to anything given to us, unwilling to let it go when the time comes to let it go or unwilling to allow it to be used as the Giver means it to be used, we stunt the growth of the soul. . . . The truth is that it is ours to thank Him for and ours to offer back to Him, ours to relinquish, ours to lose, ours to let go of—*if* we want to find our true selves, if we want real Life, if our hearts are set on glory."[27]

In the years after the terrible tragedy, Elliott taught in a seminary, spoke at conferences worldwide, and wrote many books, including a compelling biography of her husband Jim titled *Shadow of the Almighty*. Her courage and wisdom, forged in the fires of heartache, have inspired a generation of women (and men) to trust God more than ever before, no matter how difficult their circumstances may be. Like Deborah, Elisabeth Elliott earned her reputation, and God opened doors for her to use her gifts and skills.

LOOKING BACK, LOOKING UP

In the last chapter we found Gideon hiding in the winepress, and here we find Deborah leading her people in the open air under a palm tree. Both were called by God, and both were fierce and courageous leaders. They may have lived over 3,000 years ago, but their lives point to the timeless One. If we have eyes to see and ears to hear, we see the mark of Christ even in these ancient stories.

After Jesus was raised from the tomb, He appeared to His disciples and many others over the course of the next forty days. One of the most poignant encounters was on the road to Emmaus. Luke tells us that two of Jesus' disciples were going to the village about seven miles from Jerusalem. They were heartbroken because Jesus had been executed. When He approached them and asked to walk with them, they didn't realize who He was. We can hear their deep despair as one of them told Him, "We had hoped that he was the one who was going to redeem Israel" (Luke 24:21). A dead Messiah didn't fit into their understanding of God's redemption.

The two men were confused because they had heard reports that Jesus had come out of the tomb. Could He really have been resurrected . . . as He said He would be?

Jesus told them, "How foolish you are, and how slow to believe all that the prophets have spoken! Did not the Messiah have to suffer these things and then enter his glory?" (Luke 24:25–26) And the historian Luke adds, "Beginning with Moses and all the Prophets, he explained to them what was said in all the Scriptures concerning himself" (Luke 24:27).

Can you imagine that conversation? Jesus went back to the beginning of the Scriptures and showed the two men the entire sweep of God's hand in redemption. God had promised Abraham a son, and He promised to bless all the nations of the world through him. Isaac was just a sign, a symbol of the ultimate Son who would bless people of all times in all nations with forgiveness and love. In Egypt, the Passover lamb was slain so that God's people might live and be free. Jesus undoubtedly reminded the two men that He was the Lamb of God, the ultimate Passover Lamb. Jesus told them about the kings of Israel, pointing to the Creator and King of the universe. He spoke of exile and return, and the hundreds of prophecies of the long-awaited Messiah—who was speaking to them at that moment!

As they spoke, Jesus may have referred to the period after the conquest of the Promised Land. During the cycles of the judges, people walked away from God, were oppressed by their enemies, cried out to God for rescue, and were delivered after God sent a judge to free them. But that pattern wasn't limited to the past; we still see it today. Sin devastates individuals, families, communities, and nations. The enemy of our souls kills, steals, and destroys, but when we cry out to God, we experience the freedom and cleansing of forgiveness.

Jesus, then, is the greater Gideon and the greater Deborah, but there's an ironic twist. In ancient times, the judge led armies to victory over their enemies. But Jesus didn't come to *execute* judgment; He came to *bear* judgment. Again and again He told His disciples that He would be betrayed, falsely accused, tortured, and killed, but that He would rise from the grave after three days. For both Gideon and Deborah, victory over their enemies came through a miraculous military conquest. But for Jesus, victory over the enemy came through sacrifice, death, and resurrection.

In the era of the judges, God gave His people peace after victory. Today we live in the complex world between the "already" and the "not yet." At the cross, our King was paradoxically enthroned, and our task as believers is to now establish His kingdom of love, justice, and mercy "on earth as it is in heaven." But Christ's kingdom won't be fully complete until He comes again in power and glory. On that day He will come as the ultimate Judge to completely and finally right every wrong, dry every tear, humble the proud, and exalt the humble.

Some people think the Old Testament was a *failed attempt* at redemption, but Jesus described it as an *unfinished story*—one that was being completed right in front of the two men's eyes! The Messiah had finally come just as the prophets had predicted, but He came in a different way than anyone expected.

On the road to Emmaus that day, Jesus may have explained that Gideon and Deborah pointed to a future victory over an enemy, in fact, the chief enemy of mankind: sin and death. When they reached the village, the two men begged Him to stay with them. After they sat down for a meal, He broke bread and gave thanks. At that moment, they recognized it was Jesus! And then He vanished. They said to each other, "Were not our hearts burning within us while he talked with us on the road and opened the Scriptures to us?" (Luke 24:32)

People who stand in the gap have hearts that burn with joy, passion, and love when God opens their eyes to experience a taste of His beauty and power from reading the Scriptures. And all the Scriptures point to Jesus. He is the King, but He's not like any king the world has ever known. He is supremely powerful, yet as tender as a mother's touch. He is omniscient and knows everything about us—the best and the worst, yet He loves us still.

God called Gideon and Deborah to stand in the gap in their generations, to listen to His call and respond in faith. God is calling you and me to stand in the gap in our time, in our place, in our generation. When we hear His call, we too respond in faith. We take His hand, follow His directions, get involved in the messiness of people's problems, and watch God miraculously change lives. That's why Jesus—the greater Gideon and the greater Deborah—came. Don't miss the opportunity to stand with Him in the gap.

THINK ABOUT IT . . .

1. How did Deborah earn her reputation with her people?

2. Who are people you admire for their courage, wisdom, perseverance, and love? Choose one of them. What process (painful or pleasant) did that person experience to shape and deepen those qualities?

3. Do you see Barak as a wimp or a lion? Explain your answer.

4. What can we learn from Deborah's relationship with Barak?

5. If a woman feels limited by a man's insecurities, how should she respond? What strategy of communication may help him listen instead of react defensively?

6. What does it mean to have a "burning heart" for God? Do you have that kind of heart for Him? Why or why not?

7. What can you learn from the life of Deborah?

9 CALEB

. . . had a different spirit

"Now then, just as the LORD promised, he has kept me alive for forty-five years since the time he said this to Moses, while Israel moved about in the wilderness. So here I am today, eighty-five years old! I am still as strong today as the day Moses sent me out; I am just as vigorous to go out to battle now as I was then. Now give me this hill country that the LORD promised me that day. You yourself heard then that the Anakites were there and their cities were large and fortified, but, the LORD helping me, I will drive them out just as he said" (Josh. 14:10–12).

Early and late. We see Caleb as one of the heroes at the beginning of the exodus from Egypt, and decades later we see his courage and tenacity even when he is an old man. Even in his old age, he still tells Joshua, "Give me that mountain!" He didn't mean that he wanted it as a present with a nice bow on top. He wanted to fight for his share of the land! As a matter of fact, he asked Joshua to let him conquer the acreage guarded by the most powerful enemy warriors.

The story of Caleb begins as Moses led God's people out of Egypt into the desert. Moses sent twelve spies into Canaan to scout out the Promised Land. While there, two of them cut down a branch with a single cluster of grapes and carried it between them on a pole (Num. 13:23). I've never worked in a vineyard, but the grapes I see at the grocery store don't require two strong men to carry them. That must have been some cluster! I like to think the two men who took back the grapes were Joshua and Caleb. It had to be them! They were the only ones ready to convince everyone that the land was good and ready for the taking.

When they arrived back at the Israelite camp, all of the spies agreed the land was good . . . really good. But ten of them were worried about the giants that lived there—warriors that were too strong for former slaves to defeat. The crowd reacted with a mixture of excitement and fear, but their fear was taking over. Caleb stepped up and told them all, "We should go up and take possession of the land, for we can certainly do it" (Num. 13:30).

The debate intensified. Joshua and Caleb pleaded with the people to have faith in God and move forward to conquer the land. But the ten doubting spies poisoned the hearts of the people, and they were so scared they were ready to elect a new leader to take them back to Egypt.

Moses pleaded with God to forgive the unbelief of the people. God forgave them, but the consequence of their fear was that none of them would live to see the Promised Land—none but the two faith-filled men, Joshua and Caleb. God told Moses, "But because my servant Caleb has a different spirit and follows me wholeheartedly, I will bring him into the land he went to, and his descendants will inherit it" (Num. 14:24).

TASTING

God noted that Caleb had "a different spirit." What was different about him? What gave him courage when others doubted? Many factors may have contributed, but I believe Joshua and Caleb were the only two spies who tasted the blessing of God. I like to imagine Joshua and Caleb carrying that pole with the cluster of grapes back from the Promised Land. I envision Joshua in back, staring at the grapes. Boy, they look good! He can almost taste how sweet and juicy they are. Finally he grabs one and eats it, making those munching sounds you make when something tastes incredibly good.

Caleb looks back and yells, "Hey! What are you doing?" If he were Puerto Rican, he would have said, "Mira chico!" Or if he were Mexican, "Oye carnal!"

Joshua responds, "Caleb, you've got to taste this! It's so good! This is better than any fruit I've ever had in my life!"

Caleb reaches back and grabs a grape or two. Now they're both making munching sounds! If they were excited about taking the grapes home before, they're hyped now! As they continue to walk, they realize they've tasted something much more than fruit; they have had a taste of God's goodness, and there's no going back. They feel a new sensation—a warm, pure presence they've never felt before. They can see more clearly. They can count on the fulfillment of God's promise! The blinders are off. They have a new confidence. Their confidence in God fills them with purpose and new direction.

I know this story may sound a little exaggerated. But these were no ordinary grapes—this enormous cluster was a message of hope. They didn't just *observe* the "land flowing with milk and honey" and the enormous clusters of grapes. They held them in their hands and *tasted* them. Their tactile experience of God's blessing gave them confidence when others doubted . . . tasting gave them a different spirit.

A genuine experience of the goodness and greatness of God is essential to a vibrant faith. David invites us to, "Taste and see that the Lord is good" (Ps. 34:8). After Jesus' resurrection, He appeared to the disciples while Thomas was absent. When the others tried to tell Thomas they had seen the risen Christ, he simply couldn't wrap his mind around it . . . until Jesus appeared again. He didn't scold Thomas for doubting. Instead, He invited him to reach out and

A genuine experience of the goodness and greatness of God is essential to a vibrant faith.

touch Him: "Put your finger here; see my hands. Reach out your hand and put it into my side. Stop doubting and believe." That was enough for Thomas. He exclaimed, "My Lord and my God!" (John 20:27–28)

God understands that we sometimes need to touch, feel, and taste. He is not offended by our desire to experience His presence and His promises. In fact, He invites us to test Him, to taste Him, and to see for ourselves if what He says is true.

God's people spent forty years wandering in the desert. That must have been tough! It was no vacation and no adventure theme park; it was hard work in a harsh environment. It's hard for me to imagine their ordeal.

The closest I come to living in a desert is when I visit our plant church in Peru. They live in a desert with few resources; sand is everywhere. When I first visited the pastor's home, I saw a young woman sweeping the front sidewalk. I thought that was odd because she was sweeping sand. Then we went inside for a meal. The homes have no floors, so there was sand everywhere—in the kitchen, in the dining room, and in the bedrooms. After dinner the young lady came out with a bucket of water, sprinkled water on the sand, and swept again. I didn't want to sound rude, but I had to ask, "Why are you wetting the sand?"

She answered, "To keep it compact."

I then asked the question I really wanted to ask, "Why are you sweeping at all?"

She paused and smiled, "So it will look better."

That really touched me. Imagine trying to keep sand nice and smooth when people are walking all over it. Those people really worked hard to make the best of their situation. They did it with enthusiasm, grateful hearts, and a smile. What a life lesson! My heart thanks the living God whenever I think of those humble servants who are sold out for God and are making a huge difference every day in the lives of hundreds of families in the Peruvian desert.

God's people didn't make the best of their situation. He promised them a beautiful and abundant land, but they first had to spend a little time in the desert to become the people He had called them to be. From their response, we can see they weren't ready for life in the desert. The moment anything went wrong, they began to complain and whine—they repeatedly wanted to go back to Egypt and become slaves again! It's ironic that sometimes we get exactly what we don't want. That's what happens when we choose fear over faith, complaining over trust, and comfort over work.

Caleb and Joshua had "a different spirit" because they tasted the fruit and felt the blessing in their hands. To them, the Lord's promise was much more than a theory or a wish. It was a real experience.

NOT FINISHED YET

When we read about the time God's people spent wandering in the desert wilderness, we realize those were difficult years. When Moses went up Mount Sinai to receive God's law, the people began worshiping a golden calf. Over and over, they complained to Moses that they didn't have enough food or water, until God gave them enough (sometimes too much)! Their rejection of God after the report of the spies was the last straw, prompting God's judgment that they must wander the wilderness for forty more years. Eventually every adult who had walked out of Egypt and crossed the Red Sea on dry ground died, until only two were left: Joshua and Caleb.

I can imagine Joshua and Caleb watching for forty frustrating years, shaking their heads and thinking, *If only you had listened to us, you would already be enjoying God's blessings!* It's safe to say those years were difficult for the only two who had trusted God from the beginning. Yet both remained involved as part of the community. We can imagine them continually trying to convince people to trust God in the most difficult times. Instead of valuing their advice and admiring their courage, many

Instead of valuing their advice and admiring their courage, many people probably rejected them. That's what happens when you stand in the gap—not everyone wants to hear the truth.

people probably rejected them. That's what happens when you stand in the gap—not everyone wants to hear the truth.

After Moses died, God put Joshua in charge. At last a new generation of Israelites had emerged with the faith to move forward. For five years, the people of God fought, bled, died, and conquered the land God had promised them so long before. During those years, Caleb fought for his friends and neighbors to help them win the land God had given them. Finally, it was his turn. He remembered Moses' promise: "The land on which your feet have walked will be your inheritance and that of your children forever, because you have followed the LORD my God wholeheartedly" (Josh. 14:9).

The situation wasn't favorable for an old guy who was long past his prime. Caleb was eighty-five years old, and the land promised to him was full of easily defensible hills. The Anakites lived there and had no intentions of moving! They were an intimidating tribe of warriors—perhaps the descendants of "the sons of Anak," the giants who had scared the ten spies forty-five years earlier (Num. 13:33).

The challenges Caleb faced didn't faze him at all. We can almost see the intensity and determination in his face when we read his words to his old friend Joshua, "Now give me this hill country that the LORD promised me that day. You yourself heard then that the Anakites were there and their cities were large and fortified, but, the LORD helping me, I will drive them out just as he said" (Josh. 14:12).

NOT SO EASY

Many people think that God will fulfill His promises in a way that requires little or no work on our part. Wrong! Oh, sometimes God does His thing without us—He's God, so He can do that. More often, though, He lets us be His partners.

The enemy forces in the Promised Land didn't suddenly give up and leave when God's people approached. Joshua and his armies had to fight for every inch. People died to conquer the land God had promised them.

After God gave Paul the task of taking the gospel to every corner of the known world, the apostle suffered ridicule, beatings, and/or prison in almost every city he visited. He was under no illusions that fulfilling God's calling would be easy. He explained in his letter to the Colossians: "To this end I strenuously contend with all the energy Christ so powerfully works in me" (Col. 1:29). Paul contended [worked] with all the energy God gave him. He didn't call the shots on his own. He worked hard as the Holy Spirit lead him and empowered him all the way.

It was far from easy for Jesus, too. He suffered abandonment, false accusations, torture, and cruel execution—all to accomplish the purpose the Father had given Him.

Should we expect anything different? Joshua, Caleb, Paul, Jesus, and countless believers throughout the centuries have struggled and have left us many proofs of how God works His purposes in us.

Caleb was incredibly patient. For forty years he wandered with God's people in the desert. Then for five years he fought for others so they could have the land God had promised them. Throughout it all, Caleb served with a unique blend of humility and courage. When he had finished helping others conquer their land, he finally turned his attention to God's promise for himself and his family.

One thing that impresses me most about Caleb is his perseverance. Part of Caleb's "different spirit" was his attitude about what it took to see God's promises become a reality. He had no sense of entitlement. He wasn't looking for a promotion or a title. He didn't even use his old age as an excuse to take it easy. He didn't insist that all those other guys he helped acquire their land now return the favor. He didn't say, "I've done enough. I've earned this land. You need to win it for me." All he did was remind his friend Joshua, "Hey! Remember what God promised me! Let me go get it!"

Caleb was a low-maintenance guy. I like him. He just gets the job done. No drama. No whining. No complaining. No campaigning for position.

Caleb was a low-maintenance guy. I like him. He just gets the job done. No drama. No whining. No complaining. No campaigning for position. He puts his hand to the plow and doesn't look back. God, give me Calebs to work beside me! With the

Holy Spirit and a few Calebs, we can do serious damage to the forces of darkness in this world.

Too often, people see God as a waiter who exists only to give them what they want. When God uses delays and difficulties (like forty years in the desert) to deepen their dependence on Him, they complain just like the children of Israel complained. Do you know that God uses times of waiting? Do you realize that God is trying to get something out of you . . . or maybe to build something into you . . . during delays? That's why it takes so long sometimes.

Some people don't want to wait, and frankly, they don't want to work. They want immediate blessings with little or no effort! Others have a business type of relationship with God. They're willing to do their part if God will do His and bless them. Those people go to church (sometimes) and give money to God's cause (as little as they can bear), and they think God owes them. When they experience delays and difficulties, they feel cheated. They tell God, "Hey, look at all I've done for You, but You let me down!"

Caleb stood in the gap when he and Joshua brought back "the minority report" and recommended immediately conquering the Promised Land. He stood in the gap for his neighbors and friends by fighting for five years to help them win their land. And he stood in the gap for his own family when he fought for the hill country.

CLAIMING THE PROMISES

If Caleb had been like most people today, he would have bailed out as soon as things didn't go the way he hoped they would go. But he didn't give up, and he was no fool either. He knew what it would take to face the Anakites in hilly terrain. He realized it would be a tough fight—maybe the toughest of his life—but he trusted God to give him the strength to win the battles and take the land promised to him.

Caleb was faithful to his commitments, and he reminded Joshua and God of their commitments to him. He held them accountable. God doesn't mind when we remind Him of His promises to bless us, as long as we have the same kind of spirit as Caleb to trust *and* fight, pray *and* serve, believe *and* sweat.

We should align our hearts with His so we delight in the things that please Him. Then, with humility and courage, we can remind God of His promises to us.

The Bible is full of promises we can claim. Like Caleb, we should never demand that God jump through hoops to make our lives more pleasant and easy. Rather, we should align our hearts with His so we delight in the things that please Him. Then, with humility and courage, we can remind God of His promises to us. A few of those include:

- The promise that our future will be full of blessings and hope (Jer. 29:11).
- The promise that He will give us rest for our souls (Matt. 11:28–29).
- The promise that He will give us the strength to walk, run, and fly (Isa. 40:29–31).
- The promise to supply all our needs out of His vast storehouse (Phil. 4:19).
- The promise to give us wisdom in times of trial (James 1:2–8).
- The promise of eternal life to all who trust in Christ as their Savior (Rom. 6:23).
- The promise of peace when the world seems to be coming apart (John 14:27).
- The promise of forgiveness for every sin (Rom. 8:1).
- The promise that nothing can separate us from His love (Rom. 8:37–39).

Caleb was one who "wholly followed the Lord" (Josh. 14:9, 14). Only three people in the entire Old Testament are described that way: Joseph, Caleb, and Daniel. Others certainly were people who demonstrated great faith, but those three are singled out for their deep dependence on God and their tenacity to trust Him in the most difficult circumstances. Those three claimed God's promises—no matter how bad it looked for them during times of heartache, discouragement, and fear.

William Tyndale lived in a land with giant problems of a different sort, but he was one of the only people in England to recognize them. In the early sixteenth century, church services and the Bible were available only in Latin. Few people understood what was said each week in church, and they couldn't read the Scriptures in their own language in their homes. They worshiped and lived in spiritual ignorance.

Only a few years after Martin Luther launched the Protestant Reformation in Germany, Tyndale had an epiphany of his own. As he read the New Testament in Greek, he understood that salvation comes only by faith in Christ's sacrifice. This realization thrilled him, but he realized the common people of England didn't have the linguistic education he enjoyed. At that point, Tyndale had a choice: he could relax and enjoy the prestige of his church position, or he could take a bold risk to challenge the status quo. Like Caleb, Tyndale had a different spirit. But instead of "Give me that mountain," Tyndale's desire was, "Let me give them the truth of God's Word!" God gave him a passion to translate the New Testament into English so everyone in the country could hear, read, and experience the grace of God.

Tyndale was a respected church leader, so he asked the bishop of London for funds and support for his translation. The bishop turned him down. Soon Tyndale became convinced that the bishop's refusal was complete and final—not only for London, but for the church throughout the country, so he crossed the English Channel to the continent. In the German city of Worms, the same place where Luther had spoken boldly about the grace of God and was tried and convicted as a heretic, Tyndale released the first English translation of the Bible. Because of fierce opposition from English King Henry VIII, Cardinal Wolsey, Sir Thomas More, and other church leaders, Tyndale had to smuggle copies into the country. He was branded as the "master Antichrist" for his translation.

Tyndale believed the gospel of the New Testament shouldn't be confined to the learned clergy. (They weren't teaching the grace of God even though they understood the Bible in Latin.) The power of the gospel transformed Tyndale's heart as well as his actions. He realized many struggling people around him needed tangible help. Even after he knew he was being hunted for treason and heresy, he invested his life in caring for others. He visited religious refugees from England, ministered to the poor, and read the Bible in English to those who invited him for dinner.

After a decade on the run, Tyndale was betrayed by a friend and arrested by authorities in Europe who were complicit with the English king and church. He was tried, convicted, and sentenced to a torturous death at the stake. He was given an opportunity to recant, but he refused. Before he was tied to the wood, he prayed, "Lord, open the King of England's eyes!" Then the executioner strangled him and burned his body.

Tyndale left a legacy of uncommon courage and the power of God's Word. Before his arrest, he wrote that spreading the gospel through a readable translation of God's truth was more important than life itself. He was willing to sacrifice everything so that people could know God's truth and be transformed—and in fact, he gave his life for the cause.

A century later, things had changed in England to the point where King James officially sponsored a translation of the Bible into English. When his scholars studied Tyndale's work, they realized it was amazingly accurate. The Authorized King James Version of the Bible—which has been used for over 400 years—owes its clarity to William Tyndale.[28]

Clearly, Tyndale had "a different spirit" from other church leaders of his day. It took a hundred years for his countrymen to catch up to his passion for God and the Scriptures, but during that time, thousands of people found Christ because of one man's courage to stand in the gap . . . for God and for them.

HILL COUNTRY TODAY

Many people are fighting their own giants in difficult terrain. Single parents are under tremendous stress to manage time and resources to provide a stable, loving home for their kids, as they also try to resolve the pain of a broken relationship. Parents are standing in the gap for prodigal children. Many people are addicted to harmful substances and behaviors. We often think first of drugs, alcohol, sex, pornography, and gambling, but other addictions include food, shopping, television, and work—anything to self-medicate pain. Other giants in our land today include passivity, loneliness, and hopelessness. Those conditions often seem so entrenched that people can't imagine defeating them. Instead, they accept them as part of the landscape, and they try to survive under their crushing weight one more day.

A few people, though, have "a different spirit" and trust God to conquer giants in the rough terrain of their lives. Miriam is one of the most remarkable people I know. Her giants are numerous and strong, but she has had the courage to fight them with God's power. Years ago, Miriam felt completely hopeless. She used heroin and cocaine to medicate her pain and escape the horror of her life. At a critical point, our church offered her

A few people, though, have "a different spirit" and trust God to conquer giants in the rough terrain of their lives.

refuge from her chaos at our women's center, called "the farm." There, she got clean and sober, found new life in Christ, and began a journey to live in freedom and joy. As she grew in her new faith, she didn't know how much she would need to lean on God's power, wisdom, and comfort.

When Miriam became a Christian, the giants didn't vanish. In the years after she came from the farm, she suffered tragedy after tragedy. Her brother tragically drowned. Her daughter followed a path much like her mother's, one son showed no interest in God, and the other's mental illness caused perpetual problems for the family. During this incredibly stressful time, Miriam's parents became chronically sick.

Through all these trials, Miriam has had "a different spirit." She has faced her family's struggles—stresses that years before would have made her try to escape into drugs—with supernatural strength, hope, and gratitude. Her children have been amazed at her transformation. In fact, Miriam's influence has had a dramatic impact on her family. Her prodigal daughter came to Christ and is now a campus pastor in Camden, New Jersey, and her son is a music director leading worship at one of our campuses. Her parents' health continued to deteriorate, so she took them into her home to care for them.

In the middle of all these struggles and blessings, Miriam has experienced significant health problems and had to undergo a surgical procedure to stabilize the vertebrae in her neck.

Like Caleb, Miriam was tenaciously faithful as she fought battle after battle over a long period of time. Sometimes she got discouraged, but she always got back up to fight again. Her trust in God and the change in her life have amazed her family and inspired everyone who has watched her. Years ago, in the middle of her addiction, the circle of her life was reduced to a dot. She was completely self-absorbed. Today she is a true servant. People sense her genuine compassion. She has traveled to New Jersey many times to support her daughter, and people at our church know they can always count on her to help whenever they ask (and quite often, she dives in to help even before they ask).

In spite of the ongoing difficulties Miriam faces, she praises God for all the blessings He has given her. She makes no demands and displays no sense of entitlement. Instead, she serves with joy, humility, and tenacity—just like Caleb. When people ask her to tell her story, she smiles and talks about God's amazing faithfulness to her.

No matter how old you are, and no matter how big your giants may be, you can have "a different spirit" like Caleb's. You can fight your enemies with humility, determination, and persistence. Like him, you need to taste the goodness of the Lord. Then you will have courage to face the difficulties of the present and the uncertainties of the future.

If you're facing giants in your life today, and the terrain is difficult in your marriage, with your kids, or in your community, ask God to give you a spirit like Caleb's. He will gladly give you a taste of His presence so that you can fight with steadfastness.

ANOTHER MOUNTAIN, DIFFERENT GIANTS

On the night Jesus was betrayed, He faced the overwhelming challenge of fighting on a different mountain, Mount Calvary, against giants far more fierce than the Anakites—He faced the giants of sin and death. At dinner with His closest followers, He knew exactly what He was facing. John tells us, "Having loved his own who were in the world, he loved them to the end" (John 13:1). "To the end" was His death—His sinless life offered as a ransom for the sinners sitting around the table with Him that night . . . and for you and me.

A few hours later in the Garden of Gethsemane, Jesus had a taste of the excruciating spiritual, emotional, and physical pain He would soon endure on the cross. The horror almost crushed Him. He would be separated from the Father for the first and only time in eternity, and on the cross He would absorb all the hells every sinner ever deserved. All the punishment owed to us was piled on Him. He climbed the mountain and gave His all as our sacrifice so we wouldn't have to suffer the judgment we deserve.

Caleb risked his life for his family. Jesus gave His life for people who hated Him and ignored Him.

We live in a fallen world, so all of us face gaps from time to time in our own lives and in the lives of those we love. Some are as close as the suffering of the person sleeping next to us or down the hall in our homes. Other gaps that threaten us are in our communities: loneliness, gangs, drugs, violence, depression, poverty of spirit, and poverty of resources. Still others are the massive movements in culture that seek to normalize abortion and same-sex marriage, ignore immigrants, and shrug at the trade in child sex slaves.

Too often, people make one of two opposite errors in response to the gaps around them. Some assume the problems are too big, too hard, and too complex, so they focus on the promise of heaven as an escape from all the turmoil and pain. Certainly, heaven is a wonderful hope, but in the meantime God calls us to help the hurting and to stand up for truth and justice.

Certainly, heaven is a wonderful hope, but in the meantime God calls us to help the hurting and to stand up for truth and justice.

The other error is to trust that political solutions—right or left—are the only answers. Many Christians believe that electing their candidate will solve all the problems. Again, it's important to be engaged in the political realm, but politicians can't solve the problems of the heart.

The answer, then, isn't escape or political activism. It is to bring the kingdom and the cross together. In the cross of Christ, people taste the magnificent love of God. With a changed heart of forgiveness, freedom, and joy, they receive a new motivation and a new directive to make a difference in the lives of those around them. They have the hope of heaven, but they're committed to see God work to change lives *now*.

This kingdom work happens at all levels from the family to the international stage. But God's kingdom isn't like the right and left of the political spectrum. It's not based on power, but on humility, truth, and love. When Jesus' disciples argued about power and jockeyed for position, He corrected them: "The kings of the Gentiles lord it over them; and those who exercise authority over them call themselves Benefactors. But you are not to be like that. Instead, the greatest among you should be like the youngest, and the one who rules like the one who serves" (Luke 22:25–26).

The prophet Micah explained that God's values are often diametrically opposite of the world's: "He has showed you, O mortal, what is good. And what does the LORD require of you? To act justly and to love mercy and to walk humbly with your God" (Micah 6:8).

In His most famous sermon, Jesus elaborated on Micah's brief summary. The kind of people whose hearts have been transformed by grace are humble ("poor in spirit") and compassionate ("mourn"). They desire to represent God accurately ("hunger and thirst for righteousness") and to show mercy to those in need. They are sensitive to sin and quick to confess ("pure in heart"), are agents of reconciliation ("peacemakers"), and are willing to endure ridicule and persecution for the sake of Christ (Matt. 5:1–12).

People who stand in the gap aren't those who merely grit their teeth and try harder. They are men and women who have tasted the goodness and greatness of God, are amazed at His grace toward them, and are confident that the King of the universe is worthy of their loyalty, love, and obedience. They don't desert when things are hard, and they don't blindly trust in political solutions. Instead, they trust in the grace of God won on the cross and have confidence in the Spirit's power working in and through them to change lives. They combine ruthless realism about the problems with steadfast hope in a loving and powerful God. They have a strong hope in heaven, and they're active in advancing God's kingdom today. That's what it means to be a gap person.

Let the love of Jesus melt your heart and transform you from the inside out. Taste the beauty and power of the Lord, and let Him implant a different spirit in you. Only then will you have the courage and faith to stand in the gap over the long haul. Only then will you be motivated by love instead of competition. Only then will you delight in the things that thrill

God's heart. Only then will you truly be a person who stands in the gap for Christ, for those He loves, and for His cause.

THINK ABOUT IT . . .

1. Why was it important that Caleb and Joshua tasted the grapes when they were spies in Canaan? What difference did it make then? What difference did it make during the forty years in the wilderness and during the conquest of the Promised Land?

2. If you had been a spy, would you have stood with Joshua and Caleb in the minority report of faith, or would you have been fearful like the others? Explain your answer.

3. What do you think motivated Caleb during the five years he fought for the land of others before he fought for his own?

4. The spirit of our age is entitlement, entertainment, and ease. Why are those things so attractive? How do they damage true faith?

5. Caleb remembered the promise God gave him to take the hill country. What are two or three promises you are claiming at this point in your life (or that you need to claim)?

6. How would you describe Caleb's "different spirit"? Do you have this spirit? Why or why not?

7. Take some time to ask God to give you a taste of His grace and glory. What can you expect when God answers this prayer?

8. What can you learn from the life of Caleb?

9. After completing this book, what are the three most important principles, truths, or lessons you've learned?

10. In the appendix, you will find a profile of a gap person. Answer the questions and complete the evaluation.

END NOTES

1 William Goodhugh, William Cooke Taylor, *The Bible Cyclopedia*, (John W. Parker: London, 1843), 912.

2 Richard Langworth, ed., *Churchill by Himself: The Definitive Collection of Quotations* (Perseus Book Group: New York, 2008), 573.

3 Martin Luther King, Jr., "Letter from a Birmingham Jail," April 16, 1963, cited at African Studies Center, University of Pennsylvania, www.africa.upenn.edu/Articles_Gen/Letter_Birmingham.html

4 Elie Wiesel, *Night* (Hill and Wang: New York, 1958), 6–7.

5 Karen H. Jobes, *Esther: The NIV Application Commentary* (Zondervan: Grand Rapids, 1999), 43.

6 Eric Metaxas, *Bonhoeffer: Pastor, Martyr, Prophet, Spy* (Thomas Nelson: Nashville, 2010), 321.

7 "The Martyrdom of Dietrich Bonhoeffer," Travis Wright, October 22, 2013, jesusisthejustice.com/?p=4267

8 Dietrich Bonhoeffer, *Ethics* (Touchstone: New York, 1949), 61.

9 "One in six Americans lives in poverty, new census data reveals—much higher than official rate," *New York Daily News*, November6,2013,www.nydailynews.com/news/national/poverty-america-affects-residents-article-1.1508965

10 "15 Maps That Show How Americans Use Drugs," Pamela Engel, Gus Lubin and Mike Nudelman, September 26, 2013, www.businessinsider.com/15-maps-that-show-how-americans-use-drugs-2013-9

11 Prostitution Statistics, sex-crimes.laws.com

12 "11 Facts about Gangs," www.dosomething.org/tipsandtools/11-facts-about-gangs

13 Poverty Facts and Stats, www.globalissues.org/article/26/

14 "11 Facts about Human Trafficking," www.dosomething.org/tipsandtools/11-facts-about-human-trafficking

15 From American Presbyterian Mission, *Memorials of Protestant Missionaries to the Chinese* (Shanghai: American Presbyterian Mission Press, 1867).

16 2013 World Hunger Facts and Statistics, www.worldhunger.org/articles/Learn/world%20hunger%20facts%202002.htm

17 High School Dropout Statistics, www.statisticbrain.com/high-school-dropout-statistics/

18 "Obama Administration Deported Record 1.5 Million People," Corey Dade, December 24, 2012, www.npr.org/blogs/itsallpolitics/2012/12/24/167970002/obama-administration-deported-record-1-5-million-people

19 N. T. Wright, *Surprised by Hope* (HarperCollins: New York, 2008), 193.

20 Eusebius, *The Church History: Translation and Commentary by Paul L. Maier* (Kregel Publications: Grand Rapids, 2007, from the original, 324), 131.

21 For the reasons the number of Christians grew during this time, read Rodney Stark, *The Rise of Christianity: How the Obscure, Marginal Jesus Movement Became the Dominant Religious Force in the Western World in a Few Centuries* (San Francisco: HarperSanFrancisco, 1997).

22 Cited by many different authors and web sites, including www.messiah.edu/offices/intercultural/multicultural-programs/mlk/

23 Tim Keller, *The Reason for God* (Dutton: New York, 2008), 247.

24 Ascension Research Center, ascension-research.org/teresa.html

25 Corrie ten Boom, *The Hiding Place*, (Hendrickson Publishers: Peabody, Massachusetts, 1971), 50.

26 N. T. Wright, "The Easter Vocation," address in 2006, ntwrightpage.com/sermons/Easter06.htm

27 Elisabeth Elliott, *Passion and Purity* (Fleming Revell: Grand Rapids, 1984), 163–164.

28 "William Tyndale," Christian History, August, 2008, www.christianitytoday.com/ch/131christians/scholarsandscientists/tyndale.html

PROFILE OF A GAP PERSON

Rate your response to each statement on a scale of 1 to 5 on the following pages. After you complete each section, add the numbers for that characteristic to get your total.

As you answer, be honest. This is a self-evaluation tool to help you see where God is already at work in your life . . . and where He may need to do a little more to sharpen and shape you.

When you've finished scoring and adding your totals, go to the end to look at the evaluations.

A Gap Person . . .

I move toward people who are in need and try to determine how I can help.

Never	1
Rarely	2
Sometimes	3
Often	4
Always	5

I react impulsively, either to fix people's problems or to run from them.

Never	5
Rarely	4
Sometimes	3
Often	2
Always	1

When I notice genuine needs, I take time to analyze them to find the best way to help.

Not at all	1
Probably not	2
Maybe	3
Probably	4
Definitely	5

Needy people annoy me. I try to stay away from them if I can.

Never	5
Rarely	4
Sometimes	3
Often	2
Always	1

God uses me to help people who are in trouble. I have a track record of serving the poor and needy.

Not at all	1
Probably not	2
Maybe	3
Probably	4
Definitely	5

TOTAL __________

Voting is too big a hassle.

Not at all	5
Probably not	4
Maybe	3
Probably	2
Definitely	1

I'm aware of the pressing social and political issues facing our community and nation.

Not at all	1
Probably not	2
Maybe	3
Probably	4
Definitely	5

I try to convince my friends to think clearly and take stands that honor God.

Not at all	1
Probably not	2
Maybe	3
Probably	4
Definitely	5

I ask God for wisdom to know how to make a difference in the big issues confronting our society.

Never	1
Rarely	2
Sometimes	3
Often	4
Always	5

I feel helpless to change things.

Not at all	5
Probably not	4
Maybe	3
Probably	2
Definitely	1

TOTAL ________

I want God's will more than anything else in life.

Not at all	1
Probably not	2
Maybe	3
Probably	4
Definitely	5

If people observed me, they would conclude that I care much more about my reputation and my comfort than God's cause.

Never	5
Rarely	4
Sometimes	3
Often	2
Always	1

I daydream about how God might use me to accomplish great things.

Not at all	1
Probably not	2
Maybe	3
Probably	4
Definitely	5

It's easy for me to find excuses to walk away when I sense that God is asking me to do hard things.

Not at all	5
Probably not	4
Maybe	3
Probably	2
Definitely	1

My genuine prayer is, "Thy kingdom come, Thy will be done."

Never	1
Rarely	2
Sometimes	3
Often	4
Always	5

TOTAL __________

I sense that I am God's chosen, adopted, empowered child.

Not at all	1
Probably not	2
Maybe	3
Probably	4
Definitely	5

Actually, I don't think God has called me to be or do anything important.

Not at all	5
Probably not	4
Maybe	3
Probably	2
Definitely	1

People say they can see God working in me and through me.

Never	1
Rarely	2
Sometimes	3
Often	4
Always	5

God has given me a clear, compelling task to perform.

Not at all	1
Probably not	2
Maybe	3
Probably	4
Definitely	5

In the past, I had a sense of God choosing me to do something great for Him, but not anymore.

Not at all	5
Probably not	4
Maybe	3
Probably	2
Definitely	1

TOTAL __________

I steer away from poor people, addicts, prostitutes, immigrants, and others that are undesirable.

Never	5
Rarely	4
Sometimes	3
Often	2
Always	1

I can look past the surface into a person's heart.

Not at all	1
Probably not	2
Maybe	3
Probably	4
Definitely	5

God has used me to turn someone's life around.

Not at all	1
Probably not	2
Maybe	3
Probably	4
Definitely	5

I believe every person has intrinsic value, no matter how far he or she has fallen.

Not at all	1
Probably not	2
Maybe	3
Probably	4
Definitely	5

Giving money and time to poor people and addicts is a waste of resources.

Not at all	5
Probably not	4
Maybe	3
Probably	2
Definitely	1

TOTAL ___________

My philosophy is, "Go along to get along." It's best to avoid making waves.

Not at all	5
Probably not	4
Maybe	3
Probably	2
Definitely	1

I speak up about God to my family, friends, neighbors, and coworkers.

Never	1
Rarely	2
Sometimes	3
Often	4
Always	5

If the choice is between protecting my reputation or standing up for God, I choose my reputation.

Not at all	5
Probably not	4
Maybe	3
Probably	2
Definitely	1

God's values are most important to me.

Not at all	1
Probably not	2
Maybe	3
Probably	4
Definitely	5

I'm willing to take unpopular stands on social issues.

Never	1
Rarely	2
Sometimes	3
Often	4
Always	5

TOTAL ________

When I read the Bible, I sense God is actually speaking to me.

Never	1
Rarely	2
Sometimes	3
Often	4
Always	5

When I hear other people talk about a real relationship with God, I'm skeptical.

Not at all	5
Probably not	4
Maybe	3
Probably	2
Definitely	1

When I pray, I know I am in God's throne room talking to the King, who is also my Father.

Not at all	1
Probably not	2
Maybe	3
Probably	4
Definitely	5

I get nothing out of the Bible.

Never	5
Rarely	4
Sometimes	3
Often	2
Always	1

I love God. I want to know Him and serve Him even more.

Never	1
Rarely	2
Sometimes	3
Often	4
Always	5

TOTAL __________

People see me as a person they can trust.

Not at all	1
Probably not	2
Maybe	3
Probably	4
Definitely	5

My life is characterized by drift and distractions.

Never	5
Rarely	4
Sometimes	3
Often	2
Always	1

When people come to me with their problems, I ask questions and listen carefully before I offer any suggestions.

Not at all	1
Probably not	2
Maybe	3
Probably	4
Definitely	5

My prayer is very simple: "God, use me."

Never	1
Rarely	2
Sometimes	3
Often	4
Always	5

It doesn't matter what people think of me. I'm my own person, and I do what I want to do.

Never	5
Rarely	4
Sometimes	3
Often	2
Always	1

TOTAL ________

My life is characterized by spiritual joy, hope, love, and power.

Never	1
Rarely	2
Sometimes	3
Often	4
Always	5

When I serve the church and help people, I sense God's pleasure.

Never	1
Rarely	2
Sometimes	3
Often	4
Always	5

I'm more interested in my power than God's, my comfort than God using me, and my prestige than God's glory.

Not at all	5
Probably not	4
Maybe	3
Probably	2
Definitely	1

I see definite manifestations of the Spirit in my life and my worship.

Not at all	1
Probably not	2
Maybe	3
Probably	4
Definitely	5

I love to hear people tell stories of how God is using them to change lives.

Never	1
Rarely	2
Sometimes	3
Often	4
Always	5

TOTAL ________

IS MOTIVATED BY THE GOSPEL OF GOD'S GRACE

I'm amazed that God would use someone like me to meet needs and change other people's lives.

Not at all	1
Probably not	2
Maybe	3
Probably	4
Definitely	5

My obedience to God is an overflow of my love for God.

Not at all	1
Probably not	2
Maybe	3
Probably	4
Definitely	5

I've worked hard for God. I deserve much more from Him than I've gotten.

Not at all	5
Probably not	4
Maybe	3
Probably	2
Definitely	1

To me, obedience is just earning points with God. It's a grind.

Not at all	5
Probably not	4
Maybe	3
Probably	2
Definitely	1

More than anything else, I want to honor God and please Him because I've experienced His grace.

Not at all	1
Probably not	2
Maybe	3
Probably	4
Definitely	5

TOTAL __________

EVALUATION

List your score for each of the traits.

Notices problems to solve: ______
Understands the times: ______
Is "all in," no matter what the cost: ______
Is anointed by God to do His work: ______
Sees potential in people: ______
Is willing to take risks: ______
Is sensitive to the voice of God: ______
Understands God's call: ______
Has a different spirit (the Holy Spirit): ______
Is motivated by the gospel of God's grace: ______

Add your score for all 10 traits: ______

OVERALL

175 to 250 points: You're a gap person! God is either using you in a great way to stand in the gap to help people who are weak, vulnerable, and in danger, or you definitely want Him to use you!

100 to 170 points: You have significant characteristics of a person who wants to stand in the gap, but something may be lacking. Consider your motivation, training, or opportunities. Also, you may be distracted by other pursuits. Do a thorough evaluation, and make the necessary changes. Don't miss the opportunity to be God's partner in changing lives.

Below 100 points: You have some work to do—internally and externally. Take some time to pray. Ask God to refresh you with His grace and give you His heart for the needy people around you. Trust Him to give you wisdom and courage to take bold steps of faith.

SPECIFIC TRAITS

In which of the ten traits did you score 15 to 25?

Would you say those are observable, proven characteristics in your life? Explain your answer.

What are you doing now to accentuate and use those traits?

What is one thing you can do to be even more effective in each of them?

In which of the traits did you score 10 or below?

What do you need to do to become more passionate, talented, and effective in those areas?

As you evaluate your "Profile of a Gap Person," what observations do you make?

What's your next step?

USING *IN THE GAP* IN CLASSES AND GROUPS

This book is designed for individual study, small groups, and classes. The best way to absorb and apply these principles is for each person to individually study and answer the questions at the end of each chapter, then to discuss them in either a class or a group environment.

Each chapter's questions are designed to promote reflection, application, and discussion. Order enough copies of the book for each person to have a copy. For couples, encourage both to have their own book so they can record their individual reflections.

A recommended schedule for a small group or class might be:

Week 1

Introduce the material. As a group leader, tell your story of finding and fulfilling God's dream, share your hopes for the group, and provide books for each person. Encourage people to read the assigned chapter each week and answer the questions.

Weeks 2–10

Each week, introduce the topic for the week and share a story of how God has used the principles in your life. In small groups, lead people through a discussion of the questions at the end of the chapter. In classes, teach the principles in each chapter, use personal illustrations, and invite discussion.

PERSONALIZE EACH LESSON

Don't feel pressured to cover every question in your group discussions. Pick out three or four that had the greatest impact on you, and focus on those, or ask people in the group to share their responses to the questions that meant the most to them that week.

Make sure you personalize the principles and applications. At least once in each group meeting, add your own story to illustrate a particular point.

Make the Scriptures come alive. Far too often, we read the Bible like it's a phone book, with little or no emotion. Paint a vivid picture for people. Provide insights about the context of people's encounters with God, and help those in your class or group to sense the emotions of specific people in each scene.

FOCUS ON APPLICATION

The questions at the end of each chapter and your encouragement to group members to be authentic will help your group take big steps to apply the principles they're learning. Share how you are applying the principles in particular chapters each week, and encourage members to take steps of growth, too.

THREE TYPES OF QUESTIONS

If you have led groups for a few years, you already understand the importance of using open questions to stimulate discussion. Three types of questions are *limiting, leading,* and *open*. Many of the questions at the end of each lesson are open questions.

Limiting questions focus on an obvious answer, such as, "What does Jesus call Himself in John 10:11?" They don't stimulate reflection or discussion. If you want to use questions like these, follow them with thought-provoking, open questions.

Leading questions require the listener to guess what the leader has in mind, such as, "Why did Jesus use the metaphor of a shepherd in John 10?" (He was probably alluding to a passage in Ezekiel, but many people don't know that.) The teacher who asks a leading question has a definite answer in mind. Instead of asking this kind of question, you should just teach the point and perhaps ask an open question about the point you have made.

Open questions usually don't have right or wrong answers. They stimulate thinking, and they are far less threatening because the person answering doesn't risk ridicule for being wrong. These questions often begin with "Why do you think . . . ?" or "What are some reasons that . . . ?" or "How would you have felt in that situation?"

PREPARATION

As you prepare to teach this material in a group or class, consider these steps:

1. Carefully and thoughtfully read the book. Make notes, highlight key sections, quotes, or stories, and complete the reflection section at the end of each chapter. This will familiarize you with the entire scope of the content.

2. As you prepare for each week's class or group, read the corresponding chapter again and make additional notes.

3. Tailor the amount of content to the time allotted. You won't have time to cover all the questions, so pick the ones that are most pertinent.

4. Add your own stories to personalize the message and add impact.

5. Before and during your preparation, ask God to give you wisdom, clarity, and power. Trust Him to use your group to change people's lives.

6. Most people will get far more out of the group if they read the chapter and complete the reflection each week. Order books before the group or class begins or after the first week.

ABOUT THE AUTHOR

Widely known as "Pastor Choco," Wilfredo De Jesús is the Senior Pastor of New Life Covenant Church in Chicago. Under Pastor Choco's leadership, New Life Covenant is the largest church in the Assemblies of God fellowship.

Wilfredo was born and raised in Chicago's Humboldt Park community. When he was seventeen years old, he received Jesus as his Lord and Savior at a small Pentecostal Spanish-speaking church in the community. From that moment, his life was forever transformed.

He remained in that same little church for over twenty years before he was appointed Senior Pastor in July 2000. Since then, the church has grown from a weekly attendance of 120 to 17,000 globally through church plants and more than 130 ministries reaching the most disenfranchised—the brokenhearted, poor, homeless, prostitutes, drug addicts, and gang members.

Rev. De Jesús has been instrumental in the development of several community-based programs such as New Life Family Services, which operates a homeless shelter for women with children. Some of the church's other vital ministries include the Chicago Master's Commission, an intensive discipleship program for college-age students, and the Chicago Dream Center, which offers various programs and services to assist individuals and families to move toward self-sufficiency and to overcome poverty and its ill effects.

Pastor Choco's vision is simple: to be a church for the hurting that reaches people for Jesus.

In 2012, Wilfredo released his first book, *Amazing Faith,* in which he shares his life story and message: "No one is beyond the transforming power of God's love. When we let Him, God

fills our hearts with His love, strength, and purpose, and we become complete."

In April 2013, De Jesús was named one of TIME Magazine's 100 most influential people in the world and recognized for his leadership and influence with the Evangelical and Latino audiences. He wants others to understand that his accomplishments are based on a life dedicated to God and His purposes. In other words, whatever the accomplishment, to God be the glory!

De Jesús is sought after as a motivational speaker at various church events, leadership conferences, and assemblies throughout the nation and abroad. He resides in the Humboldt Park community of Chicago with his wife Elizabeth. They have three children, Alexandria, Yesenia, and Wilfredo, Jr., and a son-in-law, Anthony Gomez.

pastorwilfredodejesus

PastorChoco

OTHER RESOURCES BY WILFREDO DE JESÚS

In the Gap book (English) 978-1-93830-989-2
In the Gap ePDF (English) 978-1-93830-990-8
In the Gap epub (English) 978-1-93830-991-5
In the Gap small-group DVD (English) 978-1-62912-099-7
In the Gap study guide (English) 978-1-62912-097-3

In the Gap book (Spanish) 978-1-93830-992-2
In the Gap ePDF (Spanish) 978-1-93830-993-9
In the Gap epub (Spanish) 978-1-93830-994-6
In the Gap small-group DVD (Spanish) 978-1-62912-100-0
In the Gap study guide (Spanish) 978-1-62912-098-0

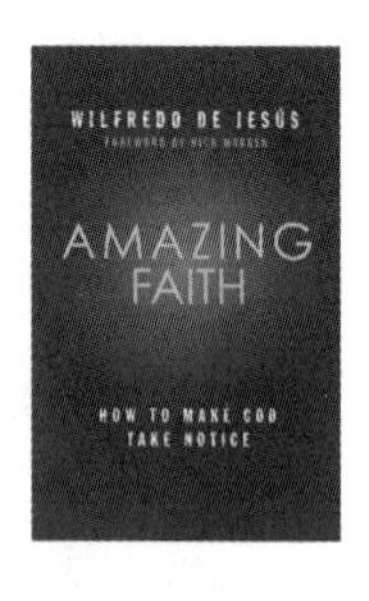

Amazing Faith book (English) 978-1-93669-995-7
Amazing Faith ePDF (English) 978-1-93669-996-4
Amazing Faith epub (English) 978-1-93669-997-1

Amazing Faith book (Spanish) 978-1-93783-058-8
Amazing Faith ePDF (Spanish) 978-1-93783-059-5
Amazing Faith epub (Spanish) 978-1-93783-060-1

For more information about these resources visit www.influenceresources.com